WORLD
HISTORY SERIES

The Holocaust

by
Michael V. Uschan

LUCENT BOOKS
An imprint of Thomson Gale, a part of The Thomson Corporation

THOMSON

GALE

Detroit • New York • San Francisco • San Diego • New Haven, Conn. • Waterville, Maine • London • Munich

LIBRARY OF CONGRESS CATALOGING-IN-PUBLICATION DATA

Uschan, Michael V., 1948–
    The Holocaust / by Michael V. Uschan.
        p. cm. — (World history series)
    Includes bibliographical references and index.
    ISBN 1-59018-252-9 (hard cover : alk. paper)
    1. Holocaust, Jewish (1939-1945)—Juvenile literature. I. Title. II. Series.
    D804.34.U83 2004
    940.53'18--dc22

                                                        2004018394

Printed in the United States of America

Contents

Foreword

Each year on the first day of school, nearly every history teacher faces the task of explaining why his or her students should study history. One logical answer to this question is that exploring what happened in our past explains how the things we often take for granted—our customs, ideas, and institutions—came to be. As statesman and historian Winston Churchill put it, "Every nation or group of nations has its own tale to tell. Knowledge of the trials and struggles is necessary to all who would comprehend the problems, perils, challenges, and opportunities which confront us today." Thus, a study of history puts modern ideas and institutions in perspective. For example, though the founders of the United States were talented and creative thinkers, they clearly did not invent the concept of democracy. Instead, they adapted some democratic ideas that had originated in ancient Greece and with which the Romans, the British, and others had experimented. An exploration of these cultures, then, reveals their very real connection to us through institutions that continue to shape our daily lives.

Another reason often given for studying history is the idea that lessons exist in the past from which contemporary societies can benefit and learn. This idea, although controversial, has always been an intriguing one for historians. Those who agree that society can benefit from the past often quote philosopher George Santayana's famous statement, "Those who cannot remember the past are condemned to repeat it." Historians who subscribe to Santayana's philosophy believe that, for example, studying the events that led up to the major world wars or other significant historical events would allow society to chart a different and more favorable course in the future.

Just as difficult as convincing students of the importance of studying history is the search for useful and interesting supplementary materials that present historical events in a context that can be easily understood. The volumes in Lucent Books' World History Series attempt to present a broad, balanced, and penetrating view of the march of history. Ancient Egypt's important wars and rulers, for example, are presented against the rich and colorful backdrop of Egyptian religious, social, and cultural developments. The series engages the reader by enhancing historical events with these cultural contexts. For example, in *Ancient Greece*, the text covers the role of women in that society. Slavery is discussed in *The Roman Empire*, as well as how slaves earned their freedom. The numerous and varied aspects of everyday life in these and other societies are explored in each volume of the series. Additionally, the series covers the major political, cultural, and philosophical ideas as the torch of civilization is passed from ancient Mesopotamia and Egypt, through Greece, Rome, Medieval Europe, and other world cultures, to the modern day.

The material in the series is formatted in a thorough, precise, and organized manner. Each volume offers the reader a comprehensive and clearly written overview of an important historical event or period. The topic under discussion is placed in a broad, historical context. For example, *The Italian Renaissance* begins with a discussion of the High Middle Ages and the loss of central control that allowed certain Italian cities to develop artistically. The book ends by looking forward to the Reformation and interpreting the societal changes that grew out of the Renaissance. Thus, students are not only involved in an historical era, but also enveloped by the events leading up to that era and the events following it.

One important and unique feature in the World History Series is the primary and secondary source quotations that richly supplement each volume. These quotes are useful in a number of ways. First, they allow students access to sources they would not normally be exposed to because of the difficulty and obscurity of the original source. The quotations range from interesting anecdotes to farsighted cultural perspectives and are drawn from historical witnesses both past and present. Second, the quotes demonstrate how and where historians themselves derive their information on the past as they strive to reach a consensus on historical events. Lastly, all of the quotes are footnoted, familiarizing students with the citation process and allowing them to verify quotes and/or look up the original source if the quote piques their interest.

Finally, the books in the World History Series provide a detailed launching point for further research. Each book contains a bibliography specifically geared toward student research. A second, annotated bibliography introduces students to all the sources the author consulted when compiling the book. A chronology of important dates gives students an overview, at a glance, of the topic covered. Where applicable, a glossary of terms is included.

In short, the series is designed not only to acquaint readers with the basics of history, but also to make them aware that their lives are a part of an ongoing human saga. Perhaps then they will come to the same realization as famed historian Arnold Toynbee. In his monumental work, *A Study of History*, he wrote about becoming aware of history flowing through him in a mighty current, and of his own life "welling like a wave in the flow of this vast tide."

Important Dates
in the History of the Holocaust

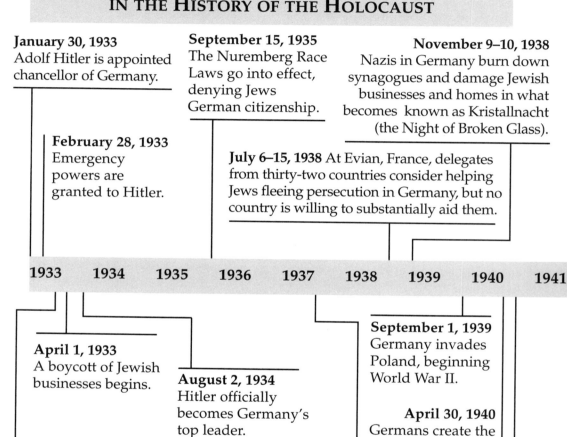

January 30, 1933
Adolf Hitler is appointed chancellor of Germany.

September 15, 1935
The Nuremberg Race Laws go into effect, denying Jews German citizenship.

November 9–10, 1938
Nazis in Germany burn down synagogues and damage Jewish businesses and homes in what becomes known as Kristallnacht (the Night of Broken Glass).

February 28, 1933
Emergency powers are granted to Hitler.

July 6–15, 1938 At Evian, France, delegates from thirty-two countries consider helping Jews fleeing persecution in Germany, but no country is willing to substantially aid them.

1933   1934   1935   1936   1937   1938   1939   1940   1941

April 1, 1933
A boycott of Jewish businesses begins.

August 2, 1934
Hitler officially becomes Germany's top leader.

September 1, 1939
Germany invades Poland, beginning World War II.

April 30, 1940
Germans create the Lodz ghetto in occupied Poland.

March 22, 1933
Dachau, Germany's first concentration camp, opens.

March 12–13, 1937
Germany annexes Austria.

May 20, 1940
The extermination camp Auschwitz is established in southern Poland.

March 24, 1933
The German parliament passes the Enabling Act, giving Hitler dictatorial powers.

June 22, 1941
Germany invades the Soviet Union.

September 29–30, 1941
SS *Einsatzgruppen* murder 33,771 Jews at Babi Yar near Kiev, Ukraine.

January 20, 1942
Top Nazi officials meet at the Wannsee Conference to plan the "Final Solution."

October 14, 1943
Six hundred Jews and Soviet prisoners of war revolt in Sobibor.

January 19, 1945
The Nazis evacuate Auschwitz and force thousands of inmates to walk to other camps.

November 20, 1945
War crimes trials begin in Nuremberg, Germany.

October 16, 1946
The first group of major Nazi war criminals found guilty in the Nuremberg Trials are executed.

December 9, 1946
Twenty-three former doctors and scientists go on trial for performing illegal medical experiments.

1941 1942 1943 1944 1945 1946 1947 1960 1962

April 19, 1943
Jews in the Warsaw ghetto begin resisting the Germans.

August 2, 1943
Two hundred Jews escape from Treblinka extermination camp during a revolt.

January 27, 1945
Soviet troops liberate Auschwitz.

April 11, 1945
U.S. soldiers liberate Buchenwald.

April 30, 1945
Hitler commits suicide in his Berlin bunker.

May 7, 1945
Germany surrenders.

May 11, 1960
Adolf Eichmann is captured in Argentina by Israeli secret service.

May 31, 1962
Eichmann is hanged.

A Twentieth-Century Horror

In the 1930s and 1940s, the Nazi regime led by Adolf Hitler murdered millions of people in an event known today as the Holocaust. The Holocaust is considered by many historians to be the twentieth century's single most terrible event. This historic mass murder of innocent people coincided with World War II, which Hitler was also responsible for starting. The chaos of war, in fact, made it easier for the Nazis to kill so many people. Primo Levi is an Italian Jew who survived a Nazi extermination camp, a facility whose main purpose was to kill people. In *The Drowned and the Saved*, Levi describes the Holocaust:

> In no other place and time has one seen a phenomenon so unexpected and so complex; never were so many human lives extinguished in so short a time, and with so lucid a combination of technological ingenuity, fanaticism and cruelty.[1]

VICTIMS OF THE HOLOCAUST

The Holocaust took the lives of 11 million men, women, and children in a mere dozen years. More than half of those killed—6 million people—were Jews; two-thirds of Europe's Jewish population prior to the war were killed. The 5 million non-Jewish victims include an estimated 3 million Polish Christians and 1 million captured Russian soldiers. Other people murdered during the Holocaust were political opponents of the Nazis such as Christian religious leaders, Gypsies, Jehovah's Witnesses, beggars, Germans with physical disabilities or mental retardation, and people classified as antisocial such as homosexuals.

Jews, Gypsies, and Poles were condemned to death because the Nazis believed they were racially inferior to Germans. Members of other groups were killed because the Nazis did not approve of their lifestyle (homosexuals) or their political and personal beliefs. Jehovah's Witnesses, for example, were murdered because their religious beliefs prohibited them from swearing allegiance to Hitler.

Most of the victims were murdered in extermination camps like Auschwitz and Treblinka, which were designed to efficiently kill thousands of people each day. Not all Holocaust victims, however, died in such camps. Some were killed elsewhere. During World War II, German soldiers slaughtered at least 1 million people in Poland and other eastern European countries. Mobile killing squads rounded up victims in cities and towns, brought them to a killing ground, and shot them to death, burying their bodies where they fell. In the most infamous mass execution, in September 1941, 33,771 Jews were killed in two days at Babi Yar, a village in the Ukraine.

The magnitude and the barbarity of the mass murders the Nazis conducted so exceeded anything the world had ever seen before that it became necessary to create new terms to describe what had happened. These chilling new words were *genocide*, *Shoah*, and *Holocaust*.

TERRIBLE NEW TERMS

Genocide is the deliberate, systematic destruction of a racial, political, or cultural group. Raphael Lemkin, a Jewish lawyer from Poland, coined this word in 1943 to describe Nazi Germany's execution of Jews, Gypsies, Poles, and other people. He created it by combining *geno*, a Greek word for "race" or "tribe," and *cide*, the Latin word for "killing."

Shoah is a Hebrew word that generally means "destruction." Shoah took on a new meaning when it was used to refer to the slaying of thousands of Polish Jews after Ger-

many invaded Poland in 1939, beginning World War II. Over time, Shoah became another name to describe the Holocaust.

The most widely used name today to describe the murder of millions of people by the Nazis is Holocaust, which came into use following World War II. It is derived from *Holokauston*, a Greek word that in English means "a sacrifice consumed

Holocaust victims crowd together on wooden bunk beds at one of several Nazi extermination camps.

Female prisoners work at an extermination camp. In the years since the Holocaust, people still struggle to understand how such an event could have happened.

by fire." *Holokauston* itself is a translation of the Hebrew word *olah*, which means "a burnt offering to God." Holocaust is considered a fitting name for what happened because the bodies of millions of victims were burned in crematoriums.

HARD TO UNDERSTAND

In the decades since the Holocaust, scholars, historians, and people everywhere have struggled to understand how it happened. One such person is Elie Wiesel, a Jew who survived imprisonment in the

Auschwitz extermination camp. After being freed from the death camp, Wiesel worked tirelessly to educate the world about the Holocaust. Wiesel once admitted that even he was mystified as to how this horror had occurred:

> How was it possible? We shall never understand. Even if we managed to learn every aspect of that insane project, we will never understand it. I think I must have read all the books—memoirs, documents, scholarly essays and testimonies written on the subject. I understand it less and less.[2]

1 The Seeds of the Holocaust

The Holocaust and World War II would never have happened if Adolf Hitler had not risen to power in Germany in the early twentieth century. Hitler won control of Germany following World War I. He did so by taking advantage of the bitterness Germans felt at losing that war. Indeed, Germany endured significant economic and political problems after its military defeat. By promising to improve Germany's shattered economy and restore the country to greatness, Hitler was able to win support for the political party he headed—the National Socialist German Workers' Party, which became known as the Nazi Party. Many Germans were drawn to the Nazi Party because they believed that Hitler would be a strong leader for a nation that was weak and struggling. One former Nazi, Albert Speer, explained why his mother joined the party in 1931:

> My mother saw a [Nazi] parade in the streets of Heidelberg. The sight of discipline in a time of chaos, the impression of energy in a time of universal hopelessness, seems to have won her over. At any rate, without ever having heard a speech or read a [party] pamphlet, she joined the party.[3]

Adolf Hitler was a dynamic speaker who rose to power in Germany after World War I.

Historians believe Hitler gained political power so quickly because he tapped into powerful emotions and ideas that so many Germans were receptive to. One of those ideas involved race. Hitler claimed that people of German descent were superior to all other races and peoples. One group of people whom Hitler reserved particular contempt for was Jews. Hitler held a bitter hatred for Jews, and many Germans shared these sentiments.

A SCAPEGOAT FOR DEFEAT

In fact, widespread prejudice against Jews had existed in Germany and other European countries for hundreds of years. Because they had always been a minority, and because many people were not familiar with Judaism, Jews were viewed by much of Christian Europe as being odd or threatening. For centuries they had been treated as scapegoats; that is, when people needed someone to blame for their misfortune or bad times, they took their anger out on the Jews. At different times in history, Christians forced Jews to live in separate areas called ghettos and denied them basic rights such as being able to own land or socialize with Christians. This hatred sometimes exploded into violence in which Jews were beaten and killed.

The word *anti-Semitism* is used to describe the irrational hatred and fear of Jews. The term is based on the word *Semite*, which refers to people who originally came from southwestern Asia, mainly Jews and Arabs. Anti-Semites who followed Hitler claimed that Jews were a separate race that was inferior to Aryans, or people from Germany and other European countries such as Great Britain, France, Italy, and Scandinavia.

Germany's strong anti-Semitism played an important role in the country's history following World War I. Most Germans were angry that they had lost the war and could not understand how their army, which they had believed was the best in the world, could have been defeated. Unable to accept the truth, Germans looked for an excuse for why their military had failed.

Many Germans began to believe that the war had been lost not by its soldiers but by inept, weak-willed government officials who made mistakes in directing the war and surrendered when Germany still had the chance to win. Many people also believed that businessmen who supplied weapons and other war products had contributed to the defeat by being more interested in making profits than in securing victory. On November 18, 1919, Paul von Hindenburg, a high-ranking military leader, summed up the bitter feelings many people had when he claimed, "The German army was stabbed in the back."[4]

Indeed, the Germans were looking for a scapegoat, someone they could blame for losing the war. Even though thousands of Jews had fought bravely for Germany, many Germans began to think Jews were responsible for Germany's defeat. Germany's long history of anti-Semitism and scapegoating made it easy to pin blame on Jews because many people already considered them untrustworthy and suspect.

One of those who proclaimed this theory the loudest was Hitler. He mockingly referred to Jews as "November criminals" because Germany had surren-

HITLER'S RACIAL IDEAS

In *Mein Kampf*, Adolf Hitler provides an insight into the racial theories that led to the Holocaust. Hitler's belief that Aryans were superior to other people gave his Nazi regime the justification to enslave and kill Jews because they were inferior. In the book Hitler wrote while in prison, he claims that Aryans are far better than other races and that Germans specifically are "the highest species of humanity on this earth. . . . All the human culture, all the results of art, science and technology that we see before us today, are almost exclusively the creative product of the Aryan. [The Aryan] alone was the founder of all higher humanity, therefore representing the prototype of all that we understand by the word 'man.'"

Hitler explains in *Mein Kampf* that he became anti-Semitic during the years he lived in Vienna. The city had many Jews, and Hitler wrote that "the more [of them] I saw, the more sharply they became distinguished in my eyes from the rest of humanity." He came to believe that Jews were not only racially inferior but the enemy of Aryans and that learning to hate them was an important achievement: "Gradually I began to hate them. For me this was the time of the greatest spiritual upheaval I have ever had to go through. I had ceased to be a weak-kneed cosmopolitan and become an anti-Semite."

dered on November 11, 1918, and he constantly charged that, by contributing to the defeat, "The Jew robbed the whole nation."[5] It was Hitler's rabid anti-Semitism that first helped him become a well-known political figure.

THE MIND OF HITLER

The man who would one day rule Germany was, ironically, not German. He was born on April 20, 1889, to Alois Schickelgruber Hitler and Klara Poelzl, in Braunau am Inn, Austria. Austria and Germany share a common language—German—and also share cultural and historical ties that make Austrians and Germans very similar.

In 1907 Hitler quit school and moved to Austria's capital, Vienna, to pursue his dream of becoming a painter. Few people bought his paintings, however; Hitler lived in poverty, and was often forced to work as a common laborer. During his years in Vienna he formed many of his political and racial opinions. As Hitler wrote in *Mein Kampf* (*My Struggle*), "[In Vienna] there took shape within me a world picture and a philosophy which became the granite foundation of all my acts."[6]

MEETING HITLER

A firm handshake, the Nazi salute, a smile. The personality of Germany's dictator was not hypnotic. Physical appearance: less attractive than from a distance. Hair: dark brown, fine in texture, inclined to rustiness in front, slightly graying on the crown. Eyes: bright blue. Skin: coarse with a pinkish tinge. Mustache: slightly shot with gray. Teeth: bottom row gold-plated, which leads to the hunch that they are false. Stature: shorter than expected. Uniform: brown boots and breeches, simple brown shirt, adorned only by the Iron Cross [a war medal] and Nazi brassard [emblem]. Smile: humorless. Salute: stylized by throwing the hand back over the shoulder. Manner: pleasant, usually not at ease, knees moving back and forth nervously.

Hitler avidly studied the ideas of the many local political groups. Germany and Austria, which were then part of the Austro-Hungarian Empire, were ruled by kings. Some Vienna groups wanted to do away with such rule and have a democracy, a type of government in which every citizen has equal rights and the power to elect officials. Hitler, however, rejected democracy. He believed the best way to govern was to have a strong individual leader who wielded supreme power. That is how he would one day rule Germany.

Hitler accepted the racial theory that Aryans, especially Germans, were physically, mentally, and morally superior to Jews as well as people from Eastern European countries such as Poland and Russia, who were collectively called Slavs.

Claimed Hitler, "All who are not of good race in this world are chaff [comparatively worthless]."[7] Hitler also believed that because they were superior, Germans were entitled to *Lebensraum*, a German word that means "living space" but which to Hitler meant land that could make Germans richer. He believed Germans were so superior that they had the right to go to war and take territory away from people in neighboring countries. Decades later, the racial ideas Hitler adopted in Vienna would form the basis for World War II and the Holocaust. He even argued that persecuting Jews was a sacred task that God condoned: "I believe that I am acting in accordance with the will of the Almighty Creator; by defending myself against the Jews, I am fighting for the work of the Lord."[8]

CREATING THE NAZI PARTY

After fighting for Germany in World War I, Hitler was so bitter over its defeat that he decided to go into politics to reclaim Germany's lost glory. His quest actually began in September 1919, when Hitler was still in the army. Stationed in Munich, Germany, Hitler was ordered to investigate a new political group—the German Workers' Party—to see if it advocated threatening or controversial ideas that could hurt Germany. The assignment changed his life.

Hitler discovered that the party was a small one with just six members, a treasury totaling a few dollars, and a limited political agenda based on anti-Semitism, helping workers, and making Germany strong again. In the small, weak group, Hitler saw the chance of a lifetime for someone who wanted to enter politics— here was an opportunity to take over an existing party and make it his own. He soon became its seventh member, and in early 1920 he quit the army to take charge of the party's propaganda, a role in which he excelled. Hitler was such a dramatic and forceful speaker that crowds soon gathered to listen to his speeches.

To make more Germans aware of the party, Hitler decided to create a dramatic symbol that would be instantly recognizable. After rejecting several designs, he settled on a flag with a red background and a large white circle that had a hooked cross known as a swastika in the center. Hitler never explained why he chose that symbol, but he was ecstatic about his new creation. Wrote Hitler, "*A symbol it really is! In red*

Nazi Party members stand at attention. Hitler became a Nazi in 1920 and embraced the party's anti-Semitic and nationalist agenda.

Two homeless men seek shelter in an abandoned building in Berlin in 1922. During the 1920s, many Germans found themselves homeless and unemployed.

we see the social idea of the movement, in *white* the nationalist idea, in the *swastika* the mission of the struggle for the victory of the Aryan man."[9]

In the spring of 1920, Hitler changed the party's name to National Socialist German Workers' Party; the nickname Nazi was derived from *Nationalsozialistische*, the German word he added that stood for "national" and "socialist." Hitler's new party soon began attracting many people who were dissatisfied with life in postwar Germany.

AN UNHAPPY COUNTRY

In the 1920s, many Germans were dissatisfied with the state of their nation. In addition to hating the fact that Germany had lost, many people believed that the victorious Allies—countries that included the United States, Great Britain, and France—were treating them too harshly. Peace treaties the Allies forced Germany to sign stripped it of some territory, including 14 percent of land it had used for agriculture. The Allies also made Germany pay billions of dollars in war reparations to cover the damage the war had caused in Allied countries. The payments were so large that they weakened the German economy and caused widespread unemployment.

The Allies also forced Kaiser Wilhelm II to step down as Germany's royal leader, which upset people still loyal to him. Germany became a democracy known as the Weimar Republic, which was governed by a president and a legislature that the citizens elected. The name came from the German town where the republic's constitution was written. Many Germans hated the Weimar Republic because the new government's officials had signed the peace treaties. The republic was also unpopular because the war reparations left the national government with so little funding that it had trouble rebuilding the country's shattered economy and providing services for citizens, including benefits for unemployed workers.

Hitler took advantage of the discontent among Germans by attacking the treaties and claiming that the government was responsible for the economic problems. Those stances made him popular, as did his bold claims that he could make life better for Germans and restore the country to greatness. More and more Germans began to support Hitler because he gave them renewed pride in their country and hope for a better future. He was especially popular with young people like Theo Hupfauer, who joined the Nazi Party while he was in college. Hupfauer explained years later: "All the young men were involved [in the Nazi Party]. To me, the old line parties were too tame, too 'establishment.' They were

for old men who had lost their fire, but not for a young man ready and willing to do something."[10]

BEER HALL PUTSCH

Hitler used new recruits to fashion the Nazi Party into a military-style organization that included the *Sturmabteilung* (SA), a group of mostly former soldiers who became his private army. Officially called storm troopers, they were also referred to as "brownshirts" because of their brown uniforms. By October 1923, the party had fifteen thousand brownshirts. The brownshirts were originally intended to provide security at Nazi Party meetings, but Hitler soon ordered them to intimidate rival political parties by beating up their members or causing disturbances at their political gatherings.

In 1923 Hitler decided to use his brownshirts to achieve his ultimate goal—control of the German government. Munich, the capital of the state of Bavaria, was home to many political parties that were critical of how the Weimar Republic governed Germany. Hitler decided to stage a political revolt there with the hope of forcing the other parties to unite with the Nazis and overthrow the republic.

On the night of November 8, Hitler and six hundred brownshirts surrounded a Munich tavern where three top Bavarian government leaders were speaking to three thousand people. Hitler entered the meeting hall, leaped on a chair, fired his pistol into the air, and declared loudly, "The national revolution has begun."[11] Hitler took the officials to a back room and tried to convince them to join him in toppling the Weimar Republic. They refused. Hitler then lied to the crowd, telling it the officials were going to help him overthrow the government.

One of those in the crowd duped by Hitler's lie was Erich Ludendorff, a former general and war hero. Believing that the officials backed Hitler, he joined the uprising because he also disliked the republic. Hitler was pleased because he thought that Ludendorff's popularity would win new recruits to his side.

The next day Hitler and Ludendorff led a group of about three thousand men in a march from the tavern to government offices in the center of the city. Hitler hoped the show of force would make local officials surrender to him. However, his plan fell apart when police armed with rifles fired on marchers after they refused an order to stop. Hitler fled from the ensuing gun battle in which sixteen marchers and three policemen were killed.

Hitler was arrested two days later and charged with treason in what became known as the Beer Hall Putsch (Revolt). Although Hitler was convicted on April 1, 1924, and sentenced to five years in prison, he remained in jail only nine months. Believing that Hitler was no longer a threat because his Nazi Party had fallen in popularity, the public prosecutor's office freed him on parole on December 20.

THE NAZI PARTY GROWS

The failed government takeover almost destroyed the Nazi Party. But it convinced Hitler that instead of revolts and radical takeovers, the best way to get control of Germany was to legitimately win political power. To do this, Hitler had to begin attracting more party members so that the party could elect Nazi candidates to the Reichstag, the German national legislature.

Hitler was a tireless and inspirational speaker, and in the next few years he gained thousands of new party members by making hundreds of appearances throughout Germany. He told Germans what they wanted to hear—that they were superior to other people, that they should not have to suffer any longer under the peace treaties they hated, and that he would restore Germany to greatness. Hitler also won new supporters with *Mein Kampf*, which he wrote while in prison after the Beer Hall Putsch. The book sold fewer than ten thousand copies when it was published in 1925, but by the time World War II started in 1939 its sales had climbed to over 5 million. Hitler used money from the sale of the book and collections at public appearances to fund the party, which began to attract more and more voters. By the 1928 election the Nazi Party was still weak, however, winning only a dozen seats in the Reichstag.

But new economic problems beginning in 1929 led to a dramatic rise in unemployment, and by the early 1930s as many as 7 million Germans did not have jobs. During this period, Hitler downplayed his racist beliefs and tried to win over voters by telling them he could make their lives better by strengthening the economy. Simplistic slogans such as "Work, Freedom, and Bread" helped convince many more Germans to vote for his party.

In 1930, 107 Nazi Party members were elected to the Reichstag, making it one of the nation's most powerful parties. In

Germans salute Adolf Hitler, who was appointed German chancellor in 1933.

1932 the party drew nearly 14 million votes and won 230 Reichstag seats. Hitler ran for president in that election but lost to Paul von Hindenburg by 6 million votes. But because the political groups backing Hindenburg needed Nazi support to have a majority in the Reichstag, on January 30, 1933, Hindenburg appointed Hitler as Germany's chancellor.

NAZI EVIL

When Hitler became chancellor, he brought to the German government the Nazi philosophy he had developed over his lifetime. He would use this post to take complete control of Germany, and ultimately launch the horrific episode known as the Holocaust.

2 The Nazis Strip People of Their Rights

Historians date the start of the Holocaust to January 30, 1933, the day Adolf Hitler became chancellor of Germany. Its end came on May 7, 1945, when Germany surrendered to end World War II combat in Europe. During that period, Hitler ruled Germany with supreme authority according to a leadership concept he called the *Führerprinzip* (leader principle). According to Hitler in *Mein Kampf*, "There must be no majority decisions. Every [leader] will have advisers by his side, but *the decision will be made by one man*. [Power] can and may be borne only by *one* man, and therefore only he alone may possess the authority and right to command."[12]

Hitler used this philosophy to create a totalitarian state, one in which the government wielded supreme control over its citizens. When Hitler became chancellor, he immediately began working to secure this ultimate power by taking away rights and liberties that were guaranteed to all Germans. Denying citizens such rights made the Holocaust possible by giving his Nazi regime the power to do anything it wanted to Jews, political opponents, and others that were deemed socially undesirable.

BECOMING "DER FÜHRER"

As chancellor, Hitler was subordinate to President Paul von Hindenburg. His Nazi Party also faced opposition from Communists, Social Democrats, and other political foes. But an incident that Hitler called "a sign from heaven"[13] helped him begin seizing the total power he craved.

On the night of February 27, 1933, there was a fire in the Reichstag building in Berlin, Germany's capital. Hitler claimed the blaze was ignited by Communists who wanted to take over Germany. However, many historians believe that the Nazis set the fire themselves to win political power. Writes historian William L. Shirer, "There is enough evidence to establish beyond a reasonable doubt that it was the Nazis who planned the arson and carried it out for their own political ends."[14] This theory is backed up by Hitler's actions the very next day. Immediately following the fire, he convinced President Hindenburg to sign an emergency order called the Decree for the Protection of People and State, which suspended civil liberties guaranteed to German citizens by the constitution. The far-reaching decree allowed police to arrest and imprison anyone without a trial. It also restricted key liberties such as freedom of speech and press, permitted searches of homes and confiscation of private property, and allowed police to open mail and listen to telephone conversations.

Acting on Hitler's orders, tens of thousands of law officials, including forty thousand *Sturmabteilung* brownshirts who had been made auxiliary policemen, invaded homes and beat people up. They arrested four thousand Communists as well as hundreds of Social Democrats, Jews, and other political opponents. Many were forced to confess to phony charges that they were trying to overthrow the government. Hitler claimed the suspension of liberties was necessary so that police could stop an alleged revolt. Hindenburg consented because he feared that the Communists would use violence to seize power in Germany as they had done in Russia during World War I. Hitler's real goal, however, was to have the power to arrest people who opposed him. Many of those who were arrested were members of the German parliament who disagreed with Nazi ideas.

By March 21 when a new session of the Reichstag opened, eighty-one Communist and twenty-six Social Democrat legislators either were imprisoned or had fled Berlin. Their absence critically affected a vote on March 23 concerning a bill Hitler introduced called the Law to Remove the Distress of People and State. This bill allowed the German cabinet (top government officials Hitler had appointed) to create new laws, even laws that violated the constitution. Prior to this, only the Reichstag had the power to make laws. Hitler claimed that the change was needed to strengthen the government's fight against Communists. He needed the bill passed because at that time so many legislators who would have opposed it were not there to vote against it. In effect, their absence helped Hitler gain control of Germany.

Hitler now had the power to reshape Germany into a Nazi state. His cabinet issued laws that abolished state legislatures, assigned Nazi officials to key posts

HUMILIATING A YOUNG BOY

After Adolf Hitler came to power in 1933, many Germans began treating Jews with contempt. In Joshua M. Greene's and Shiva Kumar's Witness: Voices from the Holocaust, *Frank S. remembers racist remarks he endured as a high school student in Breslau.*

We were supposed to learn what makes the difference between a blond, blue-eyed pure Aryan and a Jew and I hated this biology teacher with a passion. He always put me up in front of the class and said, "You see, he's a Jew," and he started to describe my nose and my cheekbones, and my hair, and my features, and how to recognize a Jew. And I was very humiliated, and I hated it, and I felt terrible about the whole thing.

in state and local government, and outlawed all other political parties. By July Hitler happily declared, "The party has now become the state."[15] When Hindenburg died on August 2, Hitler succeeded him as president, giving him total control over Germany. Hitler was now called "Der Führer," the German word for "leader" and a title that acknowledged Hitler as Germany's dictator.

TAKING RIGHTS FROM JEWS

Hitler's Nazi state immediately began a campaign against Germany's 600,000 Jews, who in 1933 made up less than 1 percent of the nation's population of 65 million. The first official action came on April 1, 1933, when the government called for a boycott of Jewish businesses. Brownshirts gathered outside shops to stop customers from entering, assaulted people who defied them, and attacked Jewish owners who protested their presence.

The state-sponsored boycott surprised German Jews. Even though many Jews were aware that anti-Semitism was growing in Germany, they believed they were safe from government persecution. The boycott angered Jews like Erich Leens, a World War I veteran from Wessel. He put on his old uniform and medals and distributed leaflets to protest the boycott against his family's department store. The leaflet read: "We [war veterans] regard this action as an attack on our national and civil honor as well as a desecration of the memory of 12,000 German soldiers of the Jewish faith who gave their lives in action."[16]

The boycott lasted only a few days. It was quickly followed by several laws that began the campaign to strip Jews of all their rights. The first laws were enacted in April 1933; these barred non-Aryans from government jobs and limited the number of Jews who could attend school. They were followed by many other restrictions, including the Nuremberg Race Laws, which were approved on September 15, 1935. This set of laws defined what constituted being a Jew (anyone with one Jewish grandparent), prohibited marriage between Aryans and Jews, and denied Jews German citizenship. Over time, Jews were banned from holding many jobs and barred from all schools. It also became illegal for Jews to own land, homes, and businesses, and they were forced to sell such property to Aryans at bargain prices. Eventually, some four hundred laws and decrees were passed against Jews.

The Nazis also passed restrictions on how Jews dressed. One anti-Jewish law forced Jews to wear a six-pointed yellow star (the Star of David, the symbol of Judaism) so that everyone would know they were Jewish. If they were found in public without the star identifying them as *Juden* (German for "Jew"), they could be severely punished or even killed.

The Nazi regime even encouraged German citizens to discriminate against Jews. Business owners began barring Jews from restaurants, hotels, and other public places. Many towns posted signs that said "JEWS NOT WELCOME." To incite hatred of Jews, brownshirts led marches in communities across Germany while singing songs with ominous lyrics like "Judah [Jews] perish!" and "Arise Hitler Folk, close the ranks. We're ready

Nazis boycott a Jewish shop in 1933. In his first official action against the Jews, Hitler called for a nationwide boycott of Jewish businesses.

for the final racial struggle."[17] Marchers attacked Jews, scrawled racist slogans on synagogues, and damaged Jewish-owned shops.

Hitler's goal was to make life for Jews so miserable that they would leave the country. As Nazi official Hermann Göring gloated in November 1938, "I would not wish to be a Jew in Germany."[18] Indeed, many did not, and by late 1939 half of Germany's Jews had fled their native land.

AUSTRIAN JEWS

A similar fate awaited 200,000 Jews in Austria. After Hitler rose to power, Nazis in Austria began working to unite the two countries. They were so successful in winning supporters that on March 12, 1938, Hitler met no resistance from Austrian leaders when he annexed Austria in what became known as *Anschluss* (Union). The next day, German soldiers marched into Austria and merged the two nations.

Austrian Jews are forced to scrub a public street after the 1938 Anschluss, *or annexation of Austria.*

The event was a disaster for Austrian Jews. German troops who marched into Austrian cities were greeted by cries of "*Judah Verrecke!*" (Destroy Jews!) from huge crowds. To celebrate *Anschluss,* German Nazis and Austrian civilians defaced Jewish property with racial slurs, attacked Jews, and made them perform humiliating tasks like scrubbing streets with toothbrushes. The Austrian government immediately put into effect the same laws that had already stripped German Jews of their rights.

Austrian Jew Fred Baron was fifteen when the Nazis stormed into Vienna. He remembers how quickly life changed for Jews:

I was kicked out of high school. My father's store was closed. Bank accounts were closed, people lost their jobs. . . . Jews could not go to any public buildings or any parks. We could not go to a library or movie. We could not go into a store, except one hour a day. Even if we had money we were not allowed to buy many things, including some foods.[19]

As in Germany, the Nazis took not only the rights of Austrian Jews but their possessions. By late 1938, an estimated forty thousand homes and twenty-five thousand businesses in Austria had been "Aryanized," which meant the Jewish property had been given or sold cheaply to Aryans. The suddenness with which their lives had been destroyed so overwhelmed them that five hundred Jews committed suicide during the first month after the nations merged.

KRISTALLNACHT

The state-sponsored campaign against Jews peaked on the night of November 9, 1938, when Reinhard Heydrich, head of the German secret police, ordered the destruction of all synagogues in Germany and Austria. In a brutal assault coordinated by Nazi officials, hundreds of thousands of brownshirts, police, and civilians burned down 101 synagogues. German firemen were ordered not to put out the blazes, and stood by and watched as buildings burned. Marauders destroyed another 76 synagogues with axes and other tools. They also damaged 7,500 Jewish businesses, busting windows and looting stores and shops.

In a shocking outburst of mindless violence that lasted fifteen hours, thousands of Jews were also beaten and at least one hundred killed. Paul Oestereicher, then a young Jewish boy, remembered the brutal scene he witnessed in Berlin that night while walking with his mother: "What seemed like hundreds of men, swinging great [wooden sticks], jumped from [trucks] and began to smash up the shops all around us."[20] The shards of broken glass that littered the streets led this historic event to be called Kristallnacht, a German word usually translated as the "Night of Broken Glass."

In the weeks following Kristallnacht, the Nazis arrested thirty thousand Jews and imprisoned them without a trial. Although they were accused of being political enemies, their only "crime" was being Jewish.

TAKING AWAY THEIR FREEDOM

The German and Austrian Jews who were arrested were sent to a new kind of detention facility the Nazis created called a concentration camp, the English translation of the German word *Konzentrationslager*. While imprisoned in camps, the inmates had no legal rights and guards could do anything they wanted to humiliate or punish them.

The brutal treatment of camp inmates was documented in an article in the November 23, 1938, edition of the *News Chronicle*, a newspaper in London, England. The story described the arrival of sixty-two Jews at a camp known as Sachsenhausen. When local police turned them over to camp guards, the inmates had to run through a line of guards wielding shovels, clubs, and whips. The policemen were so sickened by the violence that many turned away. According to the article, "When it was over, twelve of the sixty-two were dead, their skulls smashed. The

KRISTALLNACHT ORDER

In November 1938 Nazi official Reinhard Heydrich laid out guidelines for the attack on Germany's Jews that became known as Kristallnacht. The text of his order can be found on A Teacher's Guide to the Holocaust Web site.

Regards: Measures against Jews tonight.

a) Only such measures may be taken which do not jeopardize German [meaning non-Jewish] life or property (for instance, burning of synagogues only if there is no danger of fires for the neighborhoods).

b) Business establishments and homes of Jews may be destroyed but not looted. The police have been instructed to supervise the execution of these directives and to arrest looters.

c) In Business streets special care is to be taken that non-Jewish establishments will be safeguarded at all cost against damage.

As soon as the events of this night permit the use of the designated officers, as many Jews, particularly wealthy ones, as the local jails will hold, are to be arrested in all districts.

A young man sweeps debris out of the streets after Kristallnacht.

others were all unconscious. The eyes of some had been knocked out, their faces flattened and shapeless."[21]

The guards would not be punished for their actions, because under German law prisoners had no rights protecting them against such behavior. In fact, it was hoped that by treating Jews in this way, they would be scared into leaving Germany and Austria. Even though most Jews were released in a few weeks after paying government fines, which were actually bribes so they could regain their freedom, inmates were treated so brutally that one thousand died before they could be freed.

Persecuting Gypsies, Homosexuals, and Christian Minorities

The Nazis targeted many other German minority groups and stripped them of their rights, as they had the Jews. Political foes, religious minorities, and those considered to have deviant lifestyles endured much suffering and hardship under the Nazi regime. For example, Gypsies, whom the Nazis considered racially inferior, were banned from owning property.

Homosexuals were also targeted because Hitler believed that such sexual conduct was immoral. The Nazi stand on homosexuals was summed up by this 1937 party declaration: "Anyone who aims at male-male or female-female sex is our enemy."[22] Hitler also opposed homosexuality because it did not allow for procreation, and he wanted the Aryan growth rate high to make Germany stronger. The Nazis ordered local police to arrest people suspected of homosexual behavior. In 1936 the Office for Combating Homosexuality was established. One of its duties was to identify homosexuals and make employers fire them for violating laws barring gay sex.

The Nazis also attacked religious minorities who refused to recite pledges to Hitler or give the Nazi salute, in which people shouted *"Sieg Heil!"* (Hail Victory!) and thrust their right hands upward at an angle. Jehovah's Witnesses, a small Christian sect, refused to do this because they believed that God was the only person they should honor. Jehovah's Witness Elizabeth Kusserow remembers how she was scorned in school because of her religion: "Every day the teacher reprimanded me for not saluting the Nazi flag [and] I wouldn't sing those horrible Nazi songs. The children laughed and on the way home from school, they pushed me and threw my books to the ground."[23] Many other Christians were also persecuted. When some Protestant and Catholic clergymen opposed them, the Nazis created phony charges and imprisoned them. In 1938 alone, more than eight hundred ministers and priests were arrested.

Attacking the Disabled

Hitler also targeted people who were mentally ill or physically disabled. Hitler's contempt for the disabled stemmed from his belief that such people were genetically defective and a financial burden to society. Hitler first began his campaign against them early in the Holocaust, in July 1933, when he passed a law to sterilize disabled people so they could not have children. In September 1939, Hitler continued his plan to eradicate Germany of disabled people and signed an order to implement a program called *Lebens unwertes Leben*, German for "lives unworthy of life."

Hitler's order created what became known as operation T-4. The program empowered doctors to examine mentally ill or disabled people and determine, as stated in the order, which "patients, considered incurable according to the best available human judgment of their state of health, can be granted a mercy killing."[24] In the next two years, thousands of disabled and mentally ill people were taken to six medical centers in Germany and Austria and killed. At first, victims were starved to death or given lethal injections of barbiturates. Later they were placed in specially equipped vans and murdered by carbon monoxide piped in from the engines. So many people were killed that the Nazis built gas crematoriums at the medical centers so they could dispose of the bodies by burning them.

Over seventy thousand people were killed in *Lebens unwertes Leben* between January 1940 and August 1941, when

Nazis arrest a Jewish man. Jews were among several groups of people that were targeted for arrest, abuse, and harassment by the Nazis.

The Nazis built these and other gas crematoriums to dispose of the bodies of people they killed.

Hitler ended it. However, during World War II Hitler would order similar programs that killed thousands of mentally ill and disabled people in other countries.

THE HOLOCAUST

Historians believe that Hitler's decision to not just deny a class of people their civil liberties but end their lives marked an important new phase in the Holocaust. Hitler was convinced that the mass murder of whole groups of people was the way he wanted to strengthen his Nazi regime. As Holocaust historian Michael Berenbaum wrote, "The murder of the handicapped was [an early indication that] killing of a magnitude as yet unimagined would take place."[25]

3 Life in Jewish Ghettos

The word *ghetto* was coined in 1516 as the name for the only area in Venice, Italy, in which Christians allowed Jews to live. Although many European cities continued to segregate Jews in ghettos for hundreds of years, the practice had disappeared by the twentieth century. After the Nazis invaded Poland on September 1, 1939, they decided to use this historic form of discrimination to isolate and control Poland's large Jewish population. On September 21, Nazi official Reinhard Heydrich issued an order authorizing ghettos that read: "The first prerequisite for the final aim [of dealing with Jews] is the concentration of the Jews from the countryside into the larger cities. This is to be carried out with all speed [and] the aim should be to establish only a few cities of concentration."[26]

Germany eventually created more than four hundred ghettos in Poland and other countries it conquered. Ghettos were virtual prisons in which Jews were sealed off from the outside world. They were places of horrific overcrowding, and residents were frequently terrorized by German soldiers and police. Epidemics of deadly illnesses swept through the ghettos, killing thousands of people. Teenagers and adults living there were forced to work as slave laborers. Their only payment was the food the Germans distributed, but the rations were of such poor quality and so small that many people starved to death.

As the months went by and conditions worsened in the ghettos, so many people began dying from lack of food and widespread disease that it became difficult to remove their bodies. In a diary he wrote about life in the Warsaw ghetto, Isaiah Trunk comments:

> All day long there were those death wagons running back and forth constantly [to collect corpses]. When you walked down the street and you looked at people they were like skeletons. They were like dead people walking and they walked until they fell and they were dead. At times, we couldn't keep up with the burying of the dead. That's how it was.[27]

For incarcerated ghetto residents, their world shrunk into a small, horrible place filled with pain, suffering, and death.

As Adolf Hitler continued to conquer other nations to make Germany bigger and more powerful, more and more ghettos came into existence. In the spring of 1940, Hitler quickly overwhelmed other

European countries such as Belgium, Denmark, France, Greece, and Norway. Hitler's insatiable appetite for territory led him to invade the Soviet Union on June 22, 1941. His powerful military swiftly captured huge sections of that nation as well as other eastern European countries, including Hungary, Romania, Lithuania, and Czechoslovakia. The Nazis set up Jewish ghettos in every area they conquered. In Amsterdam, Holland, 100,000 Jews were imprisoned; in Budapest, Hungary, 70,000; and in Salonika, Greece, 56,000. There was even a ghetto in Shanghai, China, where Hitler's Japanese allies had rounded up 10,000 Jews.

"Jewish Residential Quarters"

The Nazis sometimes referred to ghettos as *Judischer Wohnbezirk*, German for "Jewish residential quarters." In reality they were prisons. Occupants were hemmed in by barbed wire, wood, brick, and stone. In the Krakow ghetto, Germans used tombstones stolen from Jewish cemeteries to build the walls surrounding

Mourners carry away the body of a Jew who died in the ghetto. Life in the Jewish ghettos was difficult and dangerous as there was little food, water, or medicine.

the ghetto. People went in and out through entrances controlled by armed guards. Ghettos were located in the oldest, most rundown areas of their communities and often lacked paved roads, electricity, and sewage systems.

Poland, with 3.5 million Jews, had the most crowded ghettos. The Nazis forced many Jews to move from the sixteen hundred towns and cities in which they lived to just a few hundred larger communities, like the city of Warsaw. Even Jews who were already residents of communities in which ghettos were established were forced to move to the designated ghetto areas. Jews forced out of their homes were allowed to take only the possessions they could carry; everything else was confiscated.

The Polish ghettos became tremendously overcrowded. Cities such as Lodz already had large Jewish populations, but they soon grew much larger because of the arrival of Jews from smaller communities. Rosa Goldberg Katz remembers how shocked residents of the Lodz ghetto were as newcomers swelled its size to over 165,000 people: "They kept coming in—they kept sending in people. We were so overcrowded [it] was amazing. We couldn't believe our eyes."[28]

The worst crowding occurred in the Warsaw ghetto, where a half-million people were imprisoned behind an eight-foot wall topped by broken glass. They were contained in an area of just 1.3 square miles. The ghetto encompassed one-fiftieth of the space enjoyed by the 1 million Warsaw Christians, many of whom occupied the homes that the city's 350,000 Jews had been forced to vacate. The lack of space in the ghetto meant that several families had to live in one small room that usually lacked heat, running water, or a toilet. Thousands of people were forced to take shelter in warehouses, theaters, and other buildings unfit for living.

The Nazis ruled ghettos indirectly through a *Judenrat*, a council made up of Jewish leaders who had to carry out the Nazis' orders or face death. The *Judenrat* in each ghetto organized vital community services such as mail delivery, fire protection, and health care. It also distributed food the Germans provided and assigned housing. One of the *Judenrat's* most important tasks was to oversee the labor department that assigned Jews to work for the Germans.

GHETTO WORK

All of the ghetto's Jews had to work in order to stay alive. It was only by working that a ghetto resident could obtain a ration card qualifying him or her for food. Jews twelve and older usually worked in factories and shops either within or outside the ghetto. They manufactured weapons, shoes, and even fur coats for German soldiers and civilians. They baked bread to be sold to local residents, served as warehouse workers, and even sewed insignia on Nazi uniforms. In fact, the Lodz ghetto became the largest center for military production outside Germany. At its peak, an estimated 80,000 Jews in 117 factories manufactured weapons, shells, ammunition, uniforms, and other items soldiers needed for war.

Workers toiled long hours at hard, sometimes dangerous jobs. Many worked to avoid death; they believed the Germans would not kill them as long as they were productive workers. Hinda Kibort,

A Moral Dilemma

In a September 4, 1942, speech to ghetto residents (found in Wolfgang Benz's The Holocaust: A German Historian Examines the Genocide), *Lodz ghetto leader Mordechai Chaim Rumkowski explained how difficult it was for him to enforce orders from German officials.*

Yesterday I received the order to deport some twenty thousand Jews from the ghetto. If we do not do it, others will. However, we do not allow ourselves to be ruled by the thought "How many can be saved and how many lost?" but rather by the thought "How many can be saved?" We, that is my closest colleagues and I, have come to the conclusion that we must take on the responsibility of carrying out this fateful task, however difficult we might find it. I have to perform this difficult and bloody operation. . . . In front of you stands a Jew destroyed. This is indeed the most difficult order that I have had to carry out. I stretch out my broken trembling hands to you and beseech you: place your sacrificial offerings in my hands so that I can avoid any further sacrifices, so that I can save a group of one hundred thousand Jews.

Ghetto leaders watch as a Nazi guard takes away a Jewish woman.

"You Become an Animal"

Ghetto residents lived with a constant unbearable hunger. In Holocaust: A History by Deborah Dwork and Robert Jan van Pelt, Sara Grossman-Weil explains the effect hunger had on her and other people in the Lodz ghetto.

I don't think anything hurts as much as hunger. You become wild. You're not responsible for what you say and what you do. You become an animal in the full meaning of the word. You prey on others. You will steal. This is what hunger does to us. It dehumanizes you. You're not a human being any more. . . . We were always on the look-out for some food, for some crumbs. You wouldn't care to leave a crumb on the table. You would put anything into your mouth [out of fear someone else would steal it]. . . . I think they [the Germans] let us suffer from hunger, not because there was not enough food, but because this was their method of demoralizing us, of degrading us, of torturing us. These were their methods, and they implemented these methods scrupulously. . . . We were so obsessed with satisfying this terrible hunger that nothing else mattered really. There was no other topic of conversation—if there was any conversation. There was no socializing to speak of. Other than that there was nothing to live for, just some dim hope that maybe the tomorrow will be better than the today.

who was nineteen when Germans invaded Lithuania in June 1941, worked and lived in the Kovno ghetto. She said the workers believed that "As long as we were strong and useful, we could survive."[29]

German authorities often rounded up large groups of people for labor brigades. These groups performed heavy tasks outside the ghetto such as shoveling snow from city streets, cutting stone in quarries, and repairing roads. When workers marched from the ghetto to perform such jobs, they often sang mournful songs about their situation. For example, Latvian Jews sang the following lyrics:

We are the ghetto Jews,
The loneliest people on earth.
Everything we had we lost,
We have nothing left of worth.[30]

Although the work was grueling, Jews considered themselves lucky to work outside the ghetto because such jobs usually entitled them to more food under the German system of rationing. Working beyond the walls of the ghetto also gave them opportunities to buy the healthier, fresher food found in the regular markets. And for ghetto residents, getting enough food was the single most important task in their daily fight for survival.

STARVING TO DEATH IN THE GHETTO

The Nazis hardly provided residents with enough food to stay alive. For example, in 1941 the food ration in the Lodz ghetto for one person for an entire month was one and a half pounds of meat, one egg, twelve pounds of potatoes, and two ounces of cheese. In the Warsaw ghetto, food allowances were calculated by determining how many daily calories people should receive. Soldiers were entitled to 2,312 calories but Jews only 183, which was less than one-tenth of what was needed to keep a person alive, let alone one who did physical labor for much of the day. Even the meager amounts of food the Germans did authorize did not always get into the ghettos: It was often stolen by people delivering the supplies. In a March 1942 report German official Hans Biebow admitted that "for over a year now food rations have been below those approved [and are] of an inferior quality."[31]

Food obsessed ghetto residents, who were always hungry. "The only concern of people was survival and how to get your stomach full,"[32] said Henry Golde of the Plock ghetto in Lithuania. The gnawing hunger and fear of death drove some residents to desperation. Starving men and women attacked people on ghetto streets who had food, ripping it out of their hands and stuffing it in their mouths before they could be stopped. Henry Frier remembers how one Lodz ghetto man kept his son's death a secret so that he could continue to receive his

A family starves on a Warsaw ghetto street. Food rations in the ghettos were so meager that imprisoned residents often died from starvation.

son's food rations from the Germans. "He kept him in the cellar for weeks, to collect the kid's rations. I was there. I saw it. I smelled it,"[33] said Frier.

Ghetto residents often starved to death. Between July and December 1941, nearly thirty thousand people died from starvation in the Warsaw ghetto. Yet starvation was not the only cause of death in the ghetto. Filthy conditions caused by a lack of sewage disposal and the absence of garbage pickups created epidemics of diseases such as typhus, a deadly illness that killed thousands of people.

By March 1942, starvation and illness were killing five thousand people a month in the Warsaw ghetto. The sight of dead bodies awaiting pickup by burial crews became so common that passersby took little notice of them. "If there's a corpse on the street in nothing but rags, people simply walk by and avert their eyes,"[34] Marek Stok remembered about the Warsaw ghetto. He noted, however, that if the corpse had decent clothes, people would steal them to wear or sell for food.

SMUGGLING

The constant threat of starvation led ghetto residents to smuggle food into the ghetto from the outside world. The Germans strictly prohibited smuggling food into the ghettos, and smuggling was a risky enterprise. The practice undoubtedly saved lives, however. It is estimated that smuggling provided 80 percent of the food Warsaw ghetto residents ate, and constituted much of what people in other ghettos consumed.

Although a few guards accepted bribes to allow smugglers to bring food into ghettos, it was usually very difficult to get such shipments inside. The few entrances and exits into the Warsaw ghetto, for example, were all manned by armed guards. Smugglers came up with a number of ways to bypass guards: They found weak spots and holes in the barrier surrounding the ghetto to pass food through, dug long underground tunnels, and hid food in vehicles carrying other things. Wagons that transported dead bodies out of ghettos often returned laden with food—Jews who helped move the corpses had illegally purchased it while beyond the ghetto walls. Guards rarely examined these wagons because they smelled and might be contaminated by disease.

Smuggling was dangerous because people who were caught were often shot by guards. Nevertheless, many ghetto residents were willing to risk death because they were so desperate for food. In a diary about life in the Warsaw ghetto, Emanuel Ringelblum said that the execution of a smuggler never stopped such operations for long: "The smuggling never stopped for a moment. When the street was still slippery with the blood that had been spilled, other smugglers already set out, as soon as [the signal was given] that the way was clear, to carry on with the work."[35]

GHETTO CULTURE

Ghetto life was filled with such frightening incidents. To take their minds off such depressing events and lift their spirits, residents engaged in a wide variety of cultural activities. Musicians and actors performed in concerts and plays, and writers published newspa-

SMUGGLING WAS DANGEROUS

Smuggling food and other items into the ghettos was a dangerous undertaking. In Never Again: A History of the Holocaust, *by Martin Gilbert, Krulik Wilder explains his experience as a ten-year-old boy in the Piotrkow ghetto in Poland when he was caught smuggling cigarettes.*

One day I was standing on my corner selling [smuggled] cigarettes when a [Nazi policeman] with a large dog appeared. He grabbed hold of me, took all my cigarettes, and said, "Now run." I was terrified. I was sure he was going to set the dog after me. I started running as fast as I could. He used to delight in descending on the ghetto with his ferocious black dog who wreaked havoc on the helpless and terrified victims. On another occasion six [policemen] caught me with smuggled cigarettes. I thought they were going to shoot. Instead they formed a circle around me and proceeded to kick me around like a football.

pers, poems, and stories that ghetto residents avidly read.

The ghetto in Vilna, Poland, offered literary readings, public lectures, a symphony orchestra, and the Ghetto Theater, which presented a variety of entertainment. The first theater performance on January 18, 1942, featured the dramatization of a short story, a piano recital, and poetry by ghetto resident Joseph Glazman. Ghetto resident Dr. Lazar Epstein noted in his diary how the entertainment, for a brief moment, lightened the hearts of those present: "People laughed and cried. They cast off the depression that had been weighing on their spirits. The alienation that had hitherto existed among the ghetto population seemed to have been thrown off. . . . People awoke from a long, difficult dream."[36]

The Germans tolerated many social activities in the ghettos, but they prohibited schools. They believed ignorant, uneducated people would be less likely to revolt when used as slave laborers. However, underground ghetto schools flourished even though teachers and students knew they would be punished if the Nazis discovered them. This danger was always present. Ben Giladi remembers that in the Piotrkow ghetto, "Sometimes, we had to stop in the middle of a class session and disperse rapidly when [soldiers were] raiding the block."[37]

Social life was almost nonexistent in the ghettos because there were so few places people could go to have a good time. Nevertheless, young people still found ways to get together and socialize. Said Dora Eiger, who lived in the Radom ghetto in Poland, "There was a curfew in the ghetto. You couldn't go out after eight o'clock, but we sneaked through backyards [to meet], and we did a lot of laughing and talking and joking."[38]

DEPORTATION

As terrible as ghetto life was, residents feared deportation even more. In 1942 the Germans began rounding up ghetto Jews they felt were unproductive workers (such as children, sick people, and the elderly) and sending them to extermination camps. These were specialized concentration camps that were created as a means to kill people. Although the Germans claimed they were taking them to new areas where they would be more

Although cultural activities were few, street performers like this man provided some entertainment for ghetto residents.

comfortable, ghetto Jews knew better. They had learned from various sources, including a few Jews who managed to escape from the extermination camps, that deportation would lead to death.

German soldiers and police seized people for deportation by raiding ghettos, randomly grabbing people off the streets, and taking them from their homes. Anne Levy, a young child at the time, remembers how scared she and others in the Lodz ghetto were when Nazis came looking for people to deport: "Adults went to work and children and grandparents or sick people were left behind in the house. [The] Germans would come during the day, and go through the houses, whoever was left over they would take them out."[39] Levy was never caught because her father had built a secure hiding place in their apartment. Eventually, however, it became impossible for any Jew in any ghetto to evade deportation.

EMPTYING THE GHETTOS

As Heydrich's order about creating ghettos had noted, they were only a first step in accomplishing the "final aim" in dealing with Jews. When the Nazis decided in 1942 that the ultimate goal regarding Jews was to kill them all, the ghettos were no longer necessary. The Nazis decided to empty them and send all ghetto residents to concentration camps to be murdered.

In July 1942 *Judenrat* officials in each ghetto were ordered to pre-

Jews are sent from the ghetto to concentration camps. Mass deportation of ghetto residents to the camps began in July 1942.

pare residents for a series of mass deportation. Although the Nazis claimed that residents were being moved to new work areas, Jewish leaders knew the truth; they were the most difficult orders they had ever had to obey. When Jewish leader Joseph Parnes in Lvov refused, the Nazis killed him. In the Warsaw ghetto, Adam Czerniakow committed suicide by taking poison rather than comply with the order. A note he left read, "They are demanding that I kill with my own hands the children of my people. There is no other way out but to die."[40]

Most other ghetto leaders obeyed because they hoped to keep as many people alive for as long as possible. Such leaders feared that if they did not help deport the required number of people to the camps, the Nazis would punish them by killing residents on the spot. In 1942 when Jewish leader Mordechai Chaim Rumkowski agreed to surrender all of the Lodz ghetto's children and elderly, he defended his decision in a speech to residents. Said Rumkowski: "I must cut off the limbs to save the body itself."[41]

In the end, Rumkowski could not even save himself; he died in a concentration camp. By the end of 1942 the Nazis had deported 2 million Jews from ghettos, and only a few thousand of them survived. It is also estimated that 500,000 Jews in the ghettos died from starvation, disease, and brutal treatment by policemen and soldiers.

4 The Final Solution: Mass Killing Begins

Although Hitler's Nazi regime would kill two-thirds of the Jews who lived in Europe, genocide was not his original goal when he came to power. Hitler first tried to make Germany *Judenfrei* (free of Jews) by stripping Jews of their rights and making their lives so unbearable that they would leave. Even after Germany conquered most of Europe in the early years of World War II, bringing millions of more Jews under his control, Hitler still did not order their mass destruction. Instead, he and other Nazi officials toyed with possible solutions to what they termed the "Jewish Problem," including isolating Jews in a special region in eastern Europe or moving them all to the island of Madagascar.

Even the ghettos Germany created in Poland and other countries had been only a short-term solution, a convenient way to imprison Jews until Hitler decided what to do with them. But despite the fact that Jewish workers were productive, German officials found it increasingly hard to manage ghettos. Commenting on the Lodz ghetto in the summer of 1941, Nazi officer Rolf-Heinz Hoppner admitted, "There is a danger that not all the Jews can be fed anymore. . . . The most humane solution might be to finish off Jews [rather] than to let them starve to death."[42]

In 1942 top Nazi officials met at Wannsee Lake just outside Berlin to decide the fate of Jews in the vast territory they controlled, by then nearly all of Europe. The plan that emerged from the Wannsee Conference became known as the Final Solution, or in German *Endlösung*. It would become a death sentence in the next three years for millions of Jews who would die in concentration camps created solely to exterminate them.

THE WANNSEE CONFERENCE

The Wannsee Conference was held on January 20, 1942, in an elegant mansion near Berlin. Reinhard Heydrich, who headed the Reich Security Main Office, chaired the meeting, which included a dozen other top Nazi government officials. In just ninety minutes, the Nazi leaders mapped out a detailed plan to kill every Jew in Europe. The Nazis discussed how many Jews were under Nazi control—the total was estimated at 11 million—and the methods they would use to hunt them down and transport them to their deaths.

Although Hitler did not attend the meeting and no written documents proving he ordered the extermination of European Jews have survived, several bits of evidence indicate that the Final Solution came from him. The most striking evidence comes from Rudolf Höss, the Nazi army officer who commanded the concentration camp known as Auschwitz. Höss said that when he met with top Nazi official Heinrich Himmler in the summer of 1941, Himmler told him that Hitler had ordered the destruction of all Jews:

[Himmler] said in effect: "The Führer has ordered that the Jewish question be solved once and for all and that we [Nazi soldiers] are to implement that order. The Jews are the sworn enemies of the German people and [every] Jew that we can lay our hands on is to be destroyed now during the war, without exception."[43]

The thoroughness of the Final Solution is summed up in this line from notes taken at the Wannsee Conference: "In the course of the practical execution of the final solution, Europe will be combed through from west to east."[44] Indeed, the Nazis rounded up Jews and sent them to concentration camps all over

---

IN PRAISE OF MASS MURDER

Nazi leaders very rarely commented on Germany's campaign to kill Jews. But in an October 4, 1943, speech, Heinrich Himmler praised officers of the SS, the elite military branch helping to implement the Final Solution. Himmler's words are reprinted in The Holocaust: A History of the Jews of Europe During the Second World War *by Martin Gilbert.*

Amongst ourselves, for once, it shall be said quite openly, but all the same we will never speak about it in public. . . . I am referring here to [the] extermination of the Jewish people. This is one of the things that is easily said: "The Jewish people are going to be exterminated," that's what every [Nazi] Party member says. "Sure, it's in our program, elimination of the Jews, extermination—it'll be done." [But of] all those who talk like that, not one has seen it happen, not one has had to go through with it. Most of you men know what it is like to see 100 corpses side by side, or 500 or 1,000. To have stood fast through this and—except for cases of human weakness—to have stayed decent, that has made us hard. This is an unwritten and never-to-be-written page of glory in our history. . . . We had the moral right, we had the duty towards our people, to destroy this people that wanted to destroy us. All in all, however, we can say that we have carried out this most difficult of tasks in a spirit of love for our people. And we have suffered no harm to our inner being, our soul, our character.

eastern Europe, places whose names would forever live in infamy.

TRANSPORTING JEWS

The numbers involved in the Final Solution were staggering. The vast majority of Jews to be eliminated were in eastern European countries such as Poland, which according to Wannsee Conference figures had nearly 2.3 million Jews, and the Ukraine, which had nearly 3 million. The same Wannsee tallies showed that Germany and Austria had more than 170,000 Jews, France 350,000, the Netherlands 160,000, Greece nearly 70,000, and

Belgium 43,000. There were also several million more Jews in the Soviet Union and other eastern European countries. Heydrich said the total in all countries was roughly 11 million Jews.

The Nazis decided to use trains to transport Jews to death camps. Accomplishing the Final Solution was a top priority for the Nazis: Even when railroad cars were scarce or in heavy demand, Nazi officials gave precedence to shipping Jews over transporting weapons and other war matériel. Jews were usually transported in open-air cars that normally carried cattle. They were so crowded that people could not sit or lie down. Thousands of people died even

Jews are crowded into trains headed for concentration camps. Approximately 11 million Jews were sent to camps during the deportation phase of the Final Solution.

before they reached the extermination camp because of lack of food, water, and protection from the elements; they froze to death in winter and died of heatstroke in summer.

Transporting eastern European Jews was easy because most were already imprisoned in ghettos located near railroad lines. The Germans lied to Jews, telling them they were going to be resettled to new areas to work. By the end of 1942, they had nearly emptied the ghettos. It took longer to transport Jews in western European nations, however, because the Germans needed cooperation from local officials to round them up. The Germans' claim that they were simply going to resettle Jews in eastern Europe was believable because no one knew what was going on in the huge, war-torn area to the east controlled by Germany.

France had the largest Jewish population in western Europe—350,000, including more than 150,000 who had fled from Germany, Austria, and other countries to escape Nazi persecution. Although reluctant at first to deport French Jews, French police eventually helped Germans arrest and transport about 90,000 Jews. Anti-Semitism had always been strong in France, and Premier Pierre Laval once told an American official that "foreign Jews had always been a problem in France and . . . the French government was glad [Germany] gave France an opportunity to get rid of them."[45] Officials in Holland also cooperated with the Germans, allowing 107,000 of its 160,000 Jews to be taken.

Some countries, however, did not cooperate with the Nazis in their plan to exterminate the Jews of Europe. King Boris III, for example, refused to surrender Bulgaria's 48,000 Jews. Officials in Denmark protected their 5,600 Jews and even helped many of them escape to neighboring Sweden when Denmark came under German control.

DEATH CAMPS

During Hitler's reign, about fifteen thousand concentration camps were created across Europe, some of which existed for only a few months. Many of the camps specialized in housing a particular kind of prisoner, such as workers or captured soldiers. Some were created simply as holding areas where people were gathered before they were transferred to other camps. At least some inmates died at almost every one of these camps due to starvation, illness, and guard brutality. Many camps also became sites for the mass murder of thousands of inmates through shootings or the use of gas chambers. At Dachau, the first camp established in 1933, for example, over thirty-five thousand people died, including some U.S. airmen who were captured during World War II. Victims at all camps included Jews, Soviet prisoners of war (POWs), Gypsies, homosexuals, and people who resisted the Nazis.

For the Final Solution, however, the Nazis created special facilities known as death or extermination camps. These camps were Auschwitz, Belzec, Chelmno, Majdanek, Sobibor, and Treblinka. They were all located in Poland and were organized for maximum efficiency in killing people. The Nazis often boasted about this, as SS major Alfred Franke-Gricksch did in a report following his May 1943 inspection of Auschwitz: "The Auschwitz

Ravensbruck

Sachsenhausen

GERMANY

Buchenwald

Dachau

PROTECTORATE
OF
BOHEMIA-MORAVIA

Treblinka

Chelmno

Sobibor

GERMAN-
OCCUPIED
POLAND

Belzec

Auschwitz

SLOVAKIA

Large-Scale Labor Camps

Large-Scale Extermination Camps

camp plays a special role in the resolution of the Jewish question. The most advanced methods permit the execution of [many Jews] in the shortest possible time and without arousing much attention."[46]

Auschwitz was the largest camp and claimed the most lives: an estimated 1.5 million, all but 200,000 of them Jews. Built in the Polish town of Oswiecim (Auschwitz in German) in an area of almost nineteen square miles that was isolated from the public, Auschwitz included three separate major camps and many smaller facilities adjacent to the camp. At Auschwitz, inmates who were not immediately killed were used as slave labor to make weapons, synthetic fuel, and other products. The camp's major killing camp was Auschwitz II, also known as Birkenau.

Although the other death camps were smaller than Auschwitz, all six were similar in many ways. Each camp had a railroad station where people were unloaded, and each was secured by barbed wire and fences, some of them electrified to kill anyone trying to escape. Prisoners were housed in large buildings crammed with wooden bunks in which two or even three inmates slept side-by-side without enough space to even turn over. The barracks were not heated, and people suffered from the cold in winter. Outdoor toilets were crude wooden structures built over deep holes.

The camps were run by Nazi soldiers from the elite *Schutzstaffel* (SS) military units and guards from occupied countries in eastern Europe where anti-Semitism was strong. Many of the armed guards patrolled the camps on foot. Others kept watch from tall wooden towers and shot at anyone below who tried to escape or caused trouble. Auschwitz was so large that its SS contingent numbered over six thousand.

METHODS OF MASS MURDER

The camps differed in how they killed people. Chelmno loaded people into vans and piped engine exhaust containing carbon monoxide into passenger compartments. Other camps like Treblinka, which claimed 800,000 victims, including about 3,000 Gypsies, constructed sealed chambers into which huge engines pumped deadly exhaust fumes. Some of these gas chambers were quite large. Guards lured people into them by saying they were going to have showers and be disinfected to kill lice, which people thought seemed normal after a long trip in filthy railroad cars. Explained Rudolf Höss, who commanded Auschwitz: "At Auschwitz we endeavored to fool the victims into thinking that they were to go through a delousing process [to kill lice]. Of course,

Under the watchful eyes of Nazi guards, prisoners toil at a forced labor camp.

frequently they realized our true intentions and we sometimes had riots and difficulties."[47]

The means of murder at Auschwitz was a gas known as Zyklon B. The gas contained hydrocyanic acid, which killed people in about fifteen minutes. Zyklon B was a commercial product that was already being used in the camp to kill lice in clothing and disinfect living areas. The gas had worked so well killing lice that on September 3, 1941, Deputy Commander Karl Fritzsch decided to experiment with it on 850 inmates, most of them Soviet soldiers. It so effectively murdered people that Höss decided to use it in the four gas chambers at Birkenau, which could each kill six thousand people per day. It was also chosen for Belzec and Majdanek.

To promote efficiency, Birkenau constructed self-contained killing units that housed four gas chambers as well as rooms to receive victims and dispose of their bodies. In the first room, people took off their clothes and were searched for valuables, which were later given to German citizens. They then entered the gas chambers, which usually had shower

---

A REPORT ON AUSCHWITZ

From May 14 to 16, 1943, SS major Alfred Franke-Gricksch visited Auschwitz to observe how Jews were gassed to death. He wrote his findings in a report for top Nazi officials, which can be found on the Jewish Virtual Library Web site.

[The victims] descend to a long, well-built and ventilated basement, fitted with benches on the right and left. It is brightly lit, and above the benches are numbers. The prisoners are told that they are to be disinfected and washed [and that they] have to undress completely to be bathed. In order to avoid any panic or disorder, they are told to arrange their clothes neatly and leave them under a number so that they can find their things again after the bath. Everything proceeds in complete calm. They then go through a small corridor and arrive in a big basement room that resembles a shower room. In this room, there are three big pillars. Into these it is possible from above, outside the basement, to lower [Zyklon B, a poison gas]. After 300 to 400 people have gathered in this room, the doors are closed and from above containers with the [poison] are lowered into the pillars. When the containers reach the floor of the pillars, they produce certain substances that [kill] the people. [Afterward] the door on the other side is opened, leading to a lift. The hair of the corpses is cut off and the teeth are broken out (gold teeth) by qualified people (Jews).

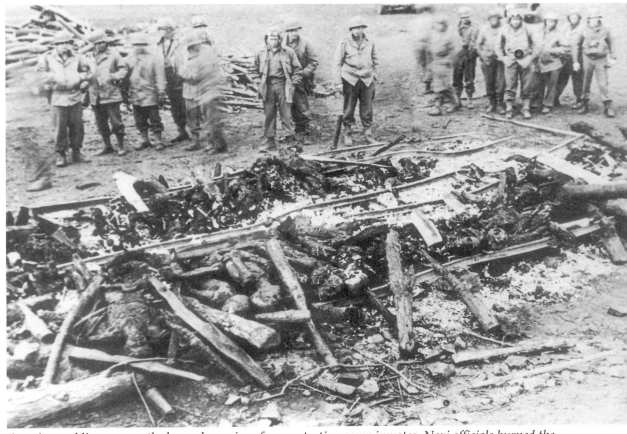

American soldiers survey the burned remains of concentration camp inmates. Nazi officials burned the bodies to make room for more victims.

heads to maintain the illusion that they were going to bathe. Depending on their size, the chambers could hold as many as one hundred people, who were usually packed tightly together. Once it was filled to capacity, instead of water, deadly gas rained down from ceiling vents. Höss described how the people died:

It could be observed through the peephole in the door that those standing nearest the vents were killed at once. The remainder staggered and began to scream and struggle for air. The screaming soon changed to the death

rattle [and] after 20 minutes at the latest no movement could be discerned.[48]

Camp inmates who had been assigned the gruesome task then stripped the dead bodies of rings, gold dental work, and any valuables they had tried to conceal from guards. The victims' hair was also cut off to make cloth and stuff mattresses and pillows.

Death camp officials soon realized they had an easier time killing people than they did disposing of their bodies. When they ran out of space to bury victims, they began burning bodies to reduce them to ashes. Early methods of burning involved piling up hundreds of bodies on layers of wood or dumping corpses in ditches and pouring fuel over them. When those methods proved to be too slow, the Germans constructed gas ovens, or crematoriums, that could incinerate hundreds of bodies each day. There were so many bodies that the ovens at Auschwitz ran almost continuously.

The use of the ovens to solve the problem of disposing of so many victims pleased Höss, who was always concerned about efficiency. Höss admitted, however, that the ovens had one drawback. The Nazis wanted to keep the mass murder of Jews as secret as possible, but the stench and heavy black smoke from the crematoriums revealed what was happening at the camp. Said Höss, "We were required to carry out these exterminations in secrecy, but of course the foul burning of bodies permeated the entire area and all the people in the [neighboring] communities knew that exterminations were going on at Auschwitz."[49]

MOBILE KILLING SQUADS

Although most of the people killed in the Holocaust died in concentration camps, they were not the only places where the Nazis committed mass murder on a scale that today still horrifies the world. The wanton slaughter of thousands of people at a time actually began on June 22, 1941, when Hitler ordered the invasion of the Soviet Union. As historian Michael Berenbaum notes, "[The invasion] marked a turning point in the Holocaust. In Soviet territory, mass killing became operational policy."[50]

During the invasion, more than 1 million Jews, as well as hundreds of thousands of Communist officials and captured Soviet soldiers, were killed in barbaric mass slayings by four *Einsatzgruppen*, military units whose sole mission was mass murder. General Otto Ohlendorf, who commanded *Einsatzgruppe D*, described his orders during his trial after World War II:

> The instructions were that . . . the Jews, as well as the Soviet political [leaders], were to be liquidated. [When asked if "liquidated" meant "killed," he replied,] "Yes, I mean 'killed.'"[51]

Each of the four *Einsatzgruppen*—designated A, B, C, and D—had 600 to 800 men who were members of SS units. The groups killed wherever they went, sometimes only a few people at one time but often by the hundreds or thousands. In July 1941 they slaughtered 5,000 Jews in Vilna, Lithuania; in August 23, 600 in Kamenets-Podolski, Ukraine; in November 19,000 in two separate incidents in Minsk, Belarus; and in November and December over 25,000 near Riga, Latvia. Although victims included Communist officials, Soviet soldiers, and some Gypsies, most were Jews.

The first mass murders occurred as the German army fought its way eastward to the Soviet Union through Latvia, Lithuania, Estonia, and the Ukraine. Following closely behind advancing soldiers, the *Einsatzgruppen* entered small communities, rounded up victims, and executed them. The most common method was to march large groups of victims into open areas like fields or forest clearings and then shoot them. Later in the war, the squads employed killing vans that piped carbon monoxide from their engines into passenger compartments, the same technique that was used to murder disabled and mentally ill people in Germany.

"ONE AFTER THE OTHER"

The most infamous mass murder occurred in September 1941 in a ravine known as Babi Yar near Kiev, the Ukraine capital. In just two days, a total of 33,771 Jews were killed by *Einsatzgruppe* soldiers and Ukrainian police. The Jews were marched from Kiev to the ravine, forced to remove their clothes and surrender valuables, and then were shot. A Ukrainian who witnessed the horrific scene described the massacre:

> Once undressed, the Jews were led into the ravine. When they reached the bottom of the ravine they were made to lie down on top of Jews who had already been shot. This all happened quickly. The corpses were literally in layers. A marksman came along and shot each Jew in the neck with a submachine gun. I saw these marksmen stand on layers of corpses and shoot one after the other.[52]

Reports that *Einsatzgruppe* officers filed about their deadly work are eerily

Nazi soldiers execute Soviet prisoners. Mass executions like these became common during Hitler's regime.

A Survivor of a Mass Shooting

Dina Pronicheva was one of a small number of Jews who survived the mass execution at Babi Yar in the Ukraine in 1941. Her account of how she escaped death can be found on the Web site A History Placed.

They lined us up on a ledge which was so small that we couldn't get much of a footing on it. They began shooting us. I shut my eyes, clenched my fists, tensed all my muscles and took a plunge down before the bullets hit me. It seemed I was flying forever. But I landed safely on the bodies. After a while, when the shooting stopped, I heard the Germans climbing into the ravine. They started finishing off all those who were not dead yet, those who were moaning, hiccuping, tossing, writhing in agony. They ran their flashlights over the bodies and finished off all who moved. I felt I was done for. I decided to keep quiet. They started covering the corpses over with earth. They must have put quite a lot over me because I felt I was beginning to suffocate. But I was afraid to move. I was gasping for breath. I knew I would suffocate. Then I decided it was better to be shot than buried alive. Using my left arm I managed to move a little way up. Then I took a deep breath, summoned up my waning strength and crawled out from under the cover of earth. It was dark. But all the same it was dangerous to crawl because of the searching beams of flashlight and they continued shooting at those who moaned. I was lucky enough to crawl up one of the high walls of the ravine, and straining every nerve and muscle, got out of it.

cold-blooded. For example, on December 1, 1941, officer Karl Jager documented that his unit had killed 133,346 Jews in Lithuania since July. "Today," Jager noted proudly, "I can confirm that our objective to solve the Jewish problem for Lithuania has been achieved."[53] More than 90 percent of Lithuanian Jews were killed in the war, the highest percentage of any country Germany occupied.

5 Life and Death in Concentration Camps

When trains pulled into Auschwitz, guards flung open the doors of cattle cars in which people were tightly jammed, forced them off with curses and blows from clubs, and herded them into the concentration camp. The Nazis called the road they walked *Himmelstrasse* (Heaven Street), a cruel joke because most were going to their death. The new arrivals formed long lines for selection, a procedure that decided who would live or die. Fred Baron, an Austrian Jew, recalls his experience with selection in 1944:

> I found myself in front of a very elegantly dressed German officer. He was wearing boots and white gloves and carried a riding whip, and with the whip he was pointing right or left, left or right. Whichever direction he pointed, guards pushed the person in front of him either left or right.[54]

Nazi SS doctors took only a few seconds to determine whether people were strong enough to perform slave labor or whether they should be sent directly to the gas chambers. The nineteen-year-old Baron was waved right, which meant life. Sent left to their deaths were people older than forty, most women, children under

fifteen, and anyone who appeared weak or ill. If the camp was crowded, there was no selection and everyone was killed.

On average, only about 10 percent of each trainload at a death camp survived this initial brush with death. Their reprieves were actually not much better since they were entering a world of terror in which most would eventually die at some point of starvation, illness and disease, or brutal treatment by guards. Concentration camp life was so terrible that many inmates would later say that being killed might have been more merciful. In 1944 Moshe Peer, an eleven-year-old French Jew, was sent to Bergen-Belsen, a labor camp in Germany, while his mother perished at Auschwitz. According to Peer, "Bergen-Belsen was worse than Auschwitz because [at Auschwitz] people were gassed right away so they didn't suffer a long time."[55]

CAMP LIFE

Although millions of people were murdered almost as soon as they entered Nazi death camps, hundreds of thousands of men, women, and children lived for long periods in the camps. Many of those inmates would eventually die from a cruel, brutal daily routine. In many ways, the purpose of camp life was to rob inmates of their health and dignity, a process that would ultimately lead to their demise.

After their arrival, inmates who survived selection were stripped of their clothes, had their heads shaved, and were given wooden-soled shoes and blue-and-white striped uniforms that were little more than worn-out rags. A series of numbers were then tattooed on their left arm. These digits became their camp identity, reducing people to a mere cipher in Nazi record books. "Within a few seconds, we had ceased to be men,"[56] author Elie Wiesel said of his arrival at Auschwitz.

Their uniforms bore inverted triangles that were color coded to identify them: green for criminals, red for political prisoners, pink for homosexuals, purple for Jehovah's Witnesses, and yellow for Jews, who wore two triangles that formed the Jewish Star of David. Non-German prisoners were further identified by the first letter of their home country, which was sewn onto their badge. The colored badges helped guards keep track of prisoners, who were usually housed by such classifications. The badges also allowed guards to easily identify Jews, Poles, and Soviet POWs, groups the Nazis singled out for the worst treatment. They were housed in the most rundown barracks, received less food, and were most often beaten or killed by guards.

Daily routine followed a tight schedule. Inmates were woken up before the sun rose and given only a few minutes to dress, wash at large sinks, use outdoor toilets, and assemble for breakfast, which they ate standing up outside. Their meal was a hunk of bread made of flour and sawdust and weak coffee or tea that tasted so horrible some could not drink it. The food they were given was often rotten or full of bugs, rendering it inedible to

THERESIENSTADT

In The World Must Know, *author Michael Berenbaum explains how the entire town of Theresienstadt, Czechoslovakia, was converted into a concentration camp. Theresienstadt became part of Nazi Germany's attempt to fool the world about how it was treating Jews.*

To quash rumors about the [camps], the Nazis permitted the visit [from the Red Cross]. But they arranged an elaborate hoax. [Theresienstadt] was beautified. Gardens were planted, houses painted, sidewalks washed, and new barracks built. A building was refitted to serve as a social center, concert hall, and synagogue. A monument was even erected to honor dead Jews. . . . The Hoax succeeded so well that a propaganda film showing how well the Jews were living under the benevolent protection of the Third Reich was made at Theresienstadt. When the filming was over, most of the cast, including nearly all of the children, were deported to Auschwitz.

all but the hungriest person. Then came a roll call in which inmates lined up by rows in a large square; this process could take hours and was particularly painful to endure in the bitter winter cold.

After breakfast, inmates went to work stations in the camp or marched to outside job sites, some of them several miles away. Prisoners labored for twelve or more hours, often without lunch. Their supper was either a cup of watery soup or more bread topped with a smear of jam and, on rare occasions, a small piece of sausage.

At night, inmates had to endure another roll call before returning to their barracks, which were filthy and infested with lice and other vermin. The bunks they slept in were so crowded that inmates had to fight to get enough space to lie down comfortably.

WORKING FOR THE SS

Prisoners entered Auschwitz under a sign that read *"Arbeit Macht Frei"* (Work Makes You Free). It was another cruel Nazi joke. No one gained their freedom by working—they gained only a reprieve from death, and not always a very long one. In the fall of 1941, for example, the Germans brought twelve thousand Soviet POWs to Auschwitz to help build Birkenau, the section where people were killed in gas chambers; within a year, all but 150 had died because of poor food, illness, brutal working conditions, and guard violence.

Work, however, was the only hope inmates had of staying alive. People who did not work were killed because they were considered useless. Inside the camps, inmates performed every job necessary to keep them running. They cleaned camp areas, including the homes of SS officers; repaired buildings, machinery, and even gas chambers and cremation ovens; kept records; and sewed prison clothing. The bitter irony of such work was that to save their own lives, they had to keep the camp operational to kill other inmates. Prisoners who were doctors and nurses worked in an inmate hospital, but there was little they could do for patients because they had almost no medical supplies to treat them. Most prisoners avoided the clinics anyway, because many who went there were slated for death by officers overseeing them.

Many prisoners became slave laborers for private businesses and government agencies. The SS, the elite Nazi military unit that ran the camps, assigned them as workers and pocketed their salaries. They were employed in nearby factories, built roads and rail lines, unloaded cargo from trains and ships, labored in rock quarries and mines, and shoveled snow. The last job was especially brutal work because inmates had no gloves or warm clothes; many froze to death or suffered such severe frostbite that they lost fingers and toes.

Slave laborers were key to Germany's military industry and helped make many weapons, including over five thousand V-2 rockets. Prisoners built these missiles in a top-secret underground facility housed in tunnels near Nordhausen, Germany. Workers lived in the nearby Dora camp or in the tunnels themselves. Some remained underground in the tunnels for months at a time. Michel Depierre, a French civilian who was captured while

Prisoners at the Buchenwald camp line up for morning roll call, a process that could last several hours.

fighting the Nazis in 1944, explained how hard he worked there:

> I was in the most cruel Hell. Twelve hours per day or night [sometimes eighteen hours] we must carry on our back extremely heavy equipment in and out of the tunnel with almost nothing in our stomach, under the rain, snow, mud, in extremely cold weather.[57]

THE *SONDERKOMMANDOS*

The most horrifying jobs were in death camps, where inmates assisted in the destruction of their fellow prisoners. The day after Abraham Jacob Krzepicki arrived at Treblinka, for example, he was taken to some railroad cars and ordered to remove the bodies of people who had died while being transported. The Jewish inmate said he was stunned by what he saw: "The mouths resembled those of dead fish. I later learned that most of these people had died of suffocation in the [overcrowded] boxcar. We, the new arrivals, were terror stricken."[58]

Krzepicki was chosen at random for that gruesome job. Some inmates, however, became members of a *Sonderkommando* (Special Command), a work group whose job was to keep the killing process going. *Sonderkommandos* were all male Jews. They led victims to the gas chambers, searched dead bodies for valuables, and loaded corpses into the ovens. Even though these inmates had to perform the horrific tasks to stay alive, it was heartbreaking for them to help murder fellow prisoners. Filip Müller, a *Sonderkommando* in Auschwitz, was once so overcome by guilt when sending Jews from his native Czechoslovakia into a gas chamber that he joined them. Said Müller:

I went into the gas chamber with them, resolved to die with them. Suddenly, some who recognized me [as a

WORK TO BREAK A PRISONER'S SPIRIT

Concentration camp guards often forced prisoners to do unnecessary work to break their spirits. In The Men with the Pink Triangles, *former inmate Heinz Heger explains the harsh, needless labor guards made homosexuals do when they first arrived at Sachsenhausen.*

In reality, the purpose was to break the very last spark of independent spirit that might possibly remain in the new prisoners by senseless yet heavy labor and to destroy the little human dignity that we still retained. . . . Our work, then, was as follows. In the morning we had to cart the snow outside our [barracks] block from the left side of the road to the right side. In the afternoon we had to cart the same snow back from the right side to the left. We didn't have [wheel]barrows and shovels to perform this work either, that would have been far too simple for us "queers." No, our [Nazi] masters had thought up something much better. We had to put our coats with the buttoned side backward, and take the snow away in the container this provided. We had to shovel up the snow with our hands—our bare hands, as we didn't have any gloves. We worked in teams of two. Twenty turns at shoveling up the snow with our hands, then twenty turns at carrying it away. And so, right through the evening, and all at the double [running very fast]! This mental and bodily torment lasted six days. Our hands were cracked all over and half frozen off, and we had become dumb and indifferent slaves of the SS.

Among the jobs camp inmates were forced to undertake was removing the dead bodies of their fellow prisoners from the transport trains.

Sonderkommando] looked at me and said, right there in the gas chamber, "So you want to die! But that is senseless. Your death won't give us back our lives. That's no way. You must get out of here alive, you must bear witness to our suffering, and to the injustice done to us."[59]

Müller survived to write about how inmates suffered in concentration camps. Of all the terrible things they endured in the camps, perhaps none was worse than the constant hunger from being slowly starved to death.

"A Starved Stomach"

Nazi records indicate that camp inmates were provided with about fifteen hundred

calories per day. In reality, however, inmates almost never got even that much because civilian contractors and the SS stole much of their food. In fact, inmates often received just eight hundred calories a day or less, well under the required daily intake of a person doing the intense physical labor that was required of most inmates. As a result, they suffered from severe malnutrition and their bodies wasted away; many looked like walking skeletons. When Zygfryd Baginski was sent to a concentration camp in 1944, the Polish Catholic weighed 220 pounds; ten months later his weight had dropped to 72 pounds. At the Aslau concentration camp in Germany where Baginski was imprisoned, many inmates suffered from hunger. Said Baginski:

One day while standing in line, I noticed a man collapse some distance away from me but in the same line. He fell against the man next to him knocking him over. We were so weak that when this man fell, one by one, like dominos, the entire line of men began falling down. I saw what was happening and I tried to step out of the way, but I was so weak that I could not move fast enough and I too went down. The SS men found this very amusing.[60]

In addition to destroying their bodies, the lack of food created a constant, gnawing hunger that dominated their existence. Jewish author Elie Wiesel explains its effect on him: "I now took little interest in anything except my daily plate of soup and my crust of stale bread. Bread, soup—these were my whole life. I was a body. Perhaps less than that even: a starved stomach. The stomach alone was aware of the passage of time."[61]

Most inmates were so hungry that they devoured every scrap of food as quickly as they could. Some, however, would save part of their morning bread to eat later in the day when they became hungry again. The danger was that someone might steal it, a calamity for a person starving to death. Food was so precious that it became the standard camp trading commodity; prisoners who still had valuables such as jewels or gold tooth fillings exchanged them for food.

Getting enough food to stay alive was hard. Inmates who worked outside the camp were more fortunate than others because they were often fed on the job by their employers and sometimes were able to bring food back to camp. Inmates lucky enough to work in the camp kitchen often got extra food as well.

Those who cleaned and did other tasks for SS personnel or their families were sometimes rewarded with extra rations for doing a good job. Desperate inmates also risked their lives by stealing food, sometimes even breaking into the kitchen or supply areas.

To better their chances of survival, several inmates or even large groups of them would band together and share any extra food they got. Judy Cohen, who was sixteen when she entered Bergen-Belsen, describes the relationship she had with Sári and Edith Feig, whom she knew from their native Hungary: "I became their lagerschwester [camp sister]. From then on, we looked after each other. The three of us shared absolutely every scrap of food. Without the help and care of [the Feigs] I would not have survived."[62]

The hunger of inmates was so overpowering that it occasionally led to incidents of cannibalism. Many prisoners remember seeing dead bodies in camp with pieces of flesh or entire limbs missing. When inmates died, other prisoners, consumed by their hunger, were driven to eat the flesh of the dead in order to save their own lives.

MEDICAL EXPERIMENTS

Another way of getting more food was to volunteer for medical experiments. Participating in Nazi-run medical experiments was extremely painful and dangerous, however, and many inmates died or were severely injured during the research. German doctors at several camps performed a wide variety of cruel experiments on inmates: They immersed

RAIDING A KITCHEN

My friend worked in the kitchen, and he said he left the window a little open and we should go at night and get some bread. We waited till late at night and pulled a board from the floor and slipped out and crossed the camp, hiding from the guards and the searchlights, and, sure enough, the kitchen window was open. We left our shoes outside and climbed in and there was so much food: potatoes, bread. I put everything in my pants, and the potatoes were hot and burned me, but I didn't care. We were leaving and I saw that they have a big pot of pea soup for the German guards. I don't know why I did it, but I pissed in the pea soup. I think "the devil made me do it." But this was the only way I could fight them. A couple of weeks later my friend said, "Let's go back," and I said, "No, the Germans are not stupid. They know we were there and they will be waiting." . . . Sure enough, my friend went back with another guy and they were caught and they beat them so terrible that you couldn't see that they were human beings. They brought the bodies to the [roll call] the next morning for everyone to see.

people in freezing cold water to see how long it took them to die, infected them with diseases such as malaria to test possible cures, shot prisoners to research how infection formed in such wounds, and tried out deadly chemicals that could be used for warfare.

The most infamous researcher was Dr. Josef Mengele, who was nicknamed the "Angel of Death" because he routinely performed selections for incoming prisoners at Auschwitz. Olga Lengyel, a prisoner-nurse at Auschwitz, remembers the strange cruelty Mengele showed after delivering an inmate's baby. "I saw him take every precaution [in the birth but] half an hour later he sent the mother and child to the crematory ovens,"[63] she said.

At Auschwitz, Mengele performed experiments on nearly fifteen hundred sets of twins; only two hundred of the three thousand survived. Mengele's experiments included infecting twins with deadly germs to see if both would die and injecting chemicals into their eyes to see if he could change the color. Vera and Olga Kriegel were only five years old when Mengele tried to find out why they had brown eyes even though their mother's were blue. Vera Kriegel said it was a painful ordeal: "They injected our eyes with liquid that burnt. But we tried to remain strong, because we knew that in Auschwitz the weak went 'up the chimney' [were cremated]."[64]

DEATH MARCHES

One of the most inhumane things the Nazis did to concentration camp inmates came in the final months of World War II, when they stubbornly and cruelly refused to surrender the prisoners to advancing Allied forces. When U.S. and other Allied soldiers neared concentration camps, the Germans transferred inmates to territory they still controlled. Instead of surren-

dering them to Allied soldiers, the Nazis herded men, women, and children out of the camps and forced them on what became known as death marches because so many of them would die.

On January 19, 1945, an estimated sixty-six thousand inmates were marched out of Auschwitz, the last surviving extermination camp; the other camps had been destroyed and even partially buried to conceal the horrors that had occurred in them. As Allied forces continued to press deeper into German territory, many other groups of prisoners began making similar deadly treks from concentration camps in the midst of winter. Their thin garments failed to protect prisoners from the cold; some inmates who did not have shoes

Nazi doctors freeze an inmate to test his response to hypothermia. Volunteering for these cruel experiments was one way inmates could avoid the gas chambers.

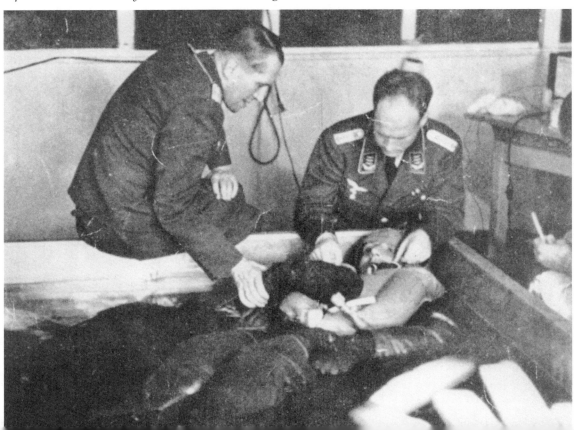

marched barefoot in the snow, often succumbing to frostbite. The marchers had little, if anything, to eat for weeks, yet their captors forced them to keep marching.

Tens of thousands of people died in the marches from the cold and starvation. And guards often shot inmates who lagged behind. Berek Latarus, a Polish Jew evacuated from Auschwitz, explained after the war how guards took stragglers aside and killed them, including his uncles who became sick and could no longer walk. "They shot all three," said Latarus. "Everybody was waiting for their turn."[65]

In early 1945 Toine de Rond, a Dutch Jew, barely escaped a similar fate when he was being moved to a camp in Germany. The final leg of the journey began on March 31, and de Rond almost did not make it. Said de Rond:

I had to walk barefoot through the snow for ten hours. Others had shoes, but not me, with my size thirteen feet. I was feverish and exhausted, and I could hardly breathe because I had tuberculosis and pneumonia. When I fell for the third time, I couldn't get up. The soldier pointed his gun at me and shouted, "Get up! I'd rather kill you than leave you here for the Allies to find!"[66]

Inmates endure a death march from Dachau. As Allied troops advanced, the Nazis marched many of their prisoners further into German-controlled areas rather than surrender them.

The soldier did not shoot him. Instead, de Rond was thrown into a cart with other sick prisoners and taken to Klarholz, Germany, where Allied soldiers freed him a few days later. Many other prisoners, however, were not as fortunate. It is estimated that 100,000 prisoners, including half of the 66,000 inmates who left Auschwitz, died in the Nazis' attempt to keep them out of the hands of advancing soldiers.

SAINT OF AUSCHWITZ

Despite the many horrors of concentration camp life, events sometimes occurred that reminded inmates of the compassion and love they had known in their previous lives. On August 14, 1941, a Polish Catholic priest named Maximilian Kolbe was one of ten Auschwitz inmates killed by an injection of poison in reprisal for the escape of a prisoner. The priest, however, had not originally been selected for death. When Kolbe saw that Polish inmate Franciszek Gajowniczek was distraught at being chosen because he had a family, Kolbe stepped forward and said, "Let me take his place. I am old. He has a wife and children."[67]

Kolbe's willingness to die for another inmate stunned those present and earned him the title "Saint of Auschwitz." Gajowniczek survived the camps and lived to be ninety-five.

6 Fighting Back: Rescuing Victims and Resisting Nazis

On October 23, 1943, Nazi sergeant Josef Schillinger was helping unload Jews from a train that had arrived at Auschwitz concentration camp. When Schillinger tried to grab the arm of one woman to hurry her along, she fought him, and the pistol he was holding fell to the ground. The woman quickly picked it up and shot him in the stomach. "Oh God, my God, what have I done that I must suffer so?"[68] Schillinger muttered as he lay on the ground dying. The woman was clubbed unconscious by other guards and taken directly to the gas chambers.

Her decision to resist the guard was one of many brave acts of individual defiance by Holocaust victims. At times, entire groups of people banded together to fight back against those who were trying to kill them. Inmates in several death camps staged revolts and mass escapes, and Jews did not always go peacefully when Nazis tried to deport them from ghettos. The largest, most famous incident of resistance occurred in the Warsaw ghetto in Poland in 1943 when poorly equipped Jewish fighters heroically battled German soldiers for nearly a month before their inevitable defeat.

Men and women in many countries, including Germany, displayed the same kind of bravery when they helped poten-

tial victims flee Nazi-occupied countries, hid them, or aided them in other ways. It took great courage to do even small things like giving food to starving concentration camp inmates. An example of one such act came in April 1945 when Christa M., a fifteen-year-old Munich girl, saw prisoners being marched from nearby Dachau. Horrified by their skeletal appearance and realizing they were starving, she began passing out cheese she had just bought:

> I had almost given it all away [when] I felt a bayonet on my back. It was [a soldier] and he screamed at me, "If you give those bastards one more piece of whatever you've got there," he said, "I'm going to make you join them! You're going to go right with them!" and I started running.[69]

Fear of such punishment kept many people from helping Holocaust victims. But some people risked being killed or imprisoned to stop the barbaric mass murder.

"THE DIFFERENCE BETWEEN LIFE AND DEATH"

Although several hundred thousand Jews fled Nazi persecution by leaving

Europe, many more could not because most countries would not allow them to legally enter their borders. This refusal was summed up by T.W. White of Australia, who said of the plight of Jews in July 1938, "It will no doubt be appreciated, that as we have no racial [that is, Jewish] problem, we are not desirous of importing one."[70]

Many historians argue whether the United States could have done more to save European Jews from the Holocaust. Even though the United States before the war allowed over 130,000 Jews to immigrate, it might have accepted many more. The U.S. Senate in February 1939 rejected a bill to grant twenty thousand Jewish children visas, the documents needed to enter America. The action prompted journalist Dorothy Thompson to write, "It is a fantastic commentary on the inhumanity of our times that for thousands and thou-sands of people a piece of paper is the difference between life and death."[71]

However, many individuals around the world did help, even when their own governments were unwilling. In the late 1930s, for example, Swiss policeman Paul Gruninger allowed about thirty-five hundred Jews to illegally enter Switzerland, where the Nazis could not hurt them. In a similar show of compassion, Sempo Sugihara, a Japanese diplomat in Kovno, Lithuania, approved thousands of visas enabling Jews to escape from Lithuania. Sugihara risked much to help these strangers, as his country was allied with Germany. After Germany conquered France, U.S. diplomat Varian Fry saved about four thousand people the Nazis were seeking. Before being arrested and sent home, Fry forged documents enabling many to leave France, and helped smuggle one thousand people to safety.

Two Jews hide in cramped quarters in Amsterdam, Holland. Many Jews tried to resist the Nazis by going into hiding.

HIDING JEWS

During the Holocaust, many men and women hid Jews from the Nazis, sometimes for several years. Jeannine Burk, for example, owes her life to a Belgian woman who sheltered her. When Germans began deporting Belgian Jews to death camps in 1942, Burk was three years old. Her father placed her with a Christian woman in Brussels, who cared for the child until 1944 when Allied soldiers liberated Belgium. For two years, the young girl had to exist in almost total isolation. Said Burk, "I lived in the house. I never went outside [where people could see her]. . . . I had no friends. [In] two years I never played with anyone."[72]

In October 1941 Austrian actress Dorothea Neff took action when she found out the Nazis were going to deport Lilli Schiff, a Jewish woman who designed her costumes. Even though Nazi officers sometimes attended parties at her apartment in Vienna, Neff hid Schiff there until May 1945, when Allied soldiers freed the Austrian capital.

People such as Neff risked much when they extended such help to Jews: The Nazis routinely executed or sent to concentration camps anyone caught hiding Jews or helping them escape.

One of the more unusual hiding places for Jews fleeing the Nazis was the Warsaw Zoo. Jan Zabinski, who headed the zoo, used empty cages to conceal hundreds of Jews and then helped them escape to safety. He even allowed about a dozen Jews to live in his home on the zoo grounds. Although it was a great risk, his efforts saved many lives.

People sometimes worked together in their rescue efforts. For example, the residents of the small French mountain village of Le Chambon-sur-Lignon banded together to save Jewish lives. Their effort began in 1941 when Andre Trocme, a Protestant minister, took in a Jewish woman fleeing the Nazis. Over the next four years, village residents fed and sheltered some five thousand Jews and helped them escape to Spain and Switzerland. Years later, a villager explained why Le Chambon-sur-Lignon residents helped: "We didn't protect the Jews because we were moral or heroic people. We helped them because it was the human thing to do."[73]

"EVERYTHING IN MY POWER"

The two most famous individuals who saved Jews from the Nazis were Oskar Schindler and Raoul Wallenberg. Unlike most rescuers who worked in secret, Schindler and Wallenberg dealt openly with the Nazis to save Jewish lives. The two men, however, employed very different methods in achieving the same goal.

Oskar Schindler was a German businessman and member of the Nazi Party. In 1939 he went to Krakow, Poland, to start a company that made German military products. His workers were Jews from the Krakow ghetto. Schindler had joined the Nazi Party to make it easier to win government contracts from Nazi officials. He did not hate Jews and respected his workers. When Schindler learned how bad living conditions were in the ghetto, he used his influence with the Nazis to allow him to house his workers at his factory, where he fed and treated them well.

ANNE FRANK

Some Jews successfully hid from the Nazis, but most were eventually discovered and sent to concentration camps. Among those discovered was the family of Anne Frank, whose story survives in a diary she wrote while hiding from the Nazis in Amsterdam, Holland. On July 6, 1942, Anne, her parents, and her older sister, Margot, went into hiding in a building her father and two Christian men owned. The Franks hid there with four other people until August 4, 1944, when an informer notified police about them. Anne died of typhus at Bergen-Belsen, but her father survived the camps and published her diary after the war. The following excerpt is from *The Diary of a Young Girl: The Definitive Edition*: "August 23, 1943: 'Believe me, if you've been shut up for a year and a half, it can get to be too much for you sometimes. But feelings can't be ignored, no matter how unjust or ungrateful they seem. I long to ride a bike, dance, whistle, look at the world, feel young and know that I'm free, and yet I can't let it show.'"

In June 1942 Schindler witnessed a deportation raid on the ghetto. He was shocked to see several people shot to death. The realization that the Germans intended to kill all of Krakow's Jews made him decide to save the lives of his workers. Said Schindler, "Beyond this day, no thinking person could fail to see what would happen [to Krakow Jews]. I was now resolved to do everything in my power to defeat the system."[74]

When advancing Soviet soldiers made Germans flee Krakow in September 1944, the Germans decided to send all Jews to concentration camps to be killed. Schindler again used his influence with Nazi officials to move fifteen hundred workers to a factory of his in Brinnlitz, Czechoslovakia, where they stayed until the end of the war. Grateful survivors gave Schindler a ring made out of one worker's gold dental work. Inscribed on the ring was a sentence from a Jewish holy book: "Whosoever saves a single soul, it is as if he had saved the whole world."[75]

Another person who dealt with the Nazis to save Jewish lives was Raoul Wallenberg, a wealthy Swedish banker. When the Nazis in 1944 began transporting 400,000 Hungarian Jews to death camps, the Swedish government sent Wallenberg to the Hungarian capital, Budapest, to save Jews who remained there. Swedish officials believed they could protect some Jews because Sweden was neutral in the war. Germany allowed this because it did not want to offend Sweden, for fear it would join the Allies and fight against Germany.

Wallenberg issued Swedish passports and special passes to thousands of

Hungarian Jews, thereby extending that country's protection over them. Because the Germans did not want to anger Sweden, they allowed those Jews to remain in Budapest instead of sending them to death camps. Wallenberg is believed to have saved the lives of at least 100,000 Jews by protecting them from the Nazis until the end of the war.

Jews take a ferry to Sweden to avoid capture by the Nazis.

GHETTO UPRISINGS

Many people risked their lives to save Jews because it was very difficult for the victims themselves to resist the Nazis who forced them into ghettos and transported them to death camps. Polish Jew Aizik Rottenberg explains why he and more than eight thousand Jews in the Wlodawa ghetto did not fight back in 1942 when they were deported to Sobibor: "A hundred men armed with machine guns are more powerful than an unarmed crowd."[76] They were also so weakened by ghetto life that resistance against strong, healthy soldiers would have been futile.

In several ghettos, however, Jews did fight back. When Jews in the Vilna ghetto in Lithuania learned that the Germans were going to deport them to death camps, they founded the United Partisan Organization (UPO). In a stirring speech on January 1, 1942, partisan leader Abba Kovner declared: "Hitler plans to destroy all the Jews of Europe, and the Jews of Lithuania have been chosen as the first in line. We will not be led like sheep to the slaughter! True, we are weak and defenseless, but the only reply to the murderer is revolt!"[77]

Kovner's group smuggled weapons into the ghetto and established ties to resistance groups in the city. In the summer of 1943, members of the UPO battled German soldiers when they began massive deportations to empty the ghetto. When the Germans won control of the ghetto, some fighters escaped through sewers and other routes to the countryside, where they continued to fight Nazis.

KINDERTRANSPORT

After the violence of Kristallnacht in November 1938, England began to allow the Kindertransport *(children transport). Until World War II began ten months later, about ten thousand German and Austrian children were authorized to live in England. Many children who went never saw their families again because they died in the Holocaust. One such child was Eve Nussbaum Soumerai, who was thirteen when she left her family for England. In* Daily Life During the Holocaust, *Soumerai describes her departure.*

[June 30, 1939] was a glorious summer day. Father, mother, and brother Bibi were jammed, along with hundreds of other parents and children, into a small room at a Berlin railway station. Everybody was in tears. It was supposed to be temporary—but in our hearts, we feared that it might not be so. My mother's last words were, "Look at the stars and pray," and she kept repeating, say "thank you to 'uncle and auntie' [the English couple taking her in]." My father hugged me one last time and said, "You have a beautiful smile, use it." And my little brother asked that I find him a home near me. My name was called over the loudspeaker, and I left them in that little crowded room. My new black patent leather shoes sounded like the beating of a hammer as I walked to the waiting train.

The Vilna group helped spark resistance in other ghettos. For example, it sent Chaika Grossman to her hometown of Bialystok, Poland, where she posed as a Christian and helped smuggle weapons into the ghetto. When the Germans came to empty the ghetto in August 1943, armed Jews she had helped organize battled fiercely, holding out for a week before being overwhelmed. Rather than be killed, Grossman and others fled the ghetto to keep fighting.

BATTLE FOR WARSAW

Resistance groups eventually developed in about one hundred eastern European ghettos. The largest was in Warsaw, the scene of the most powerful Jewish revolt against Nazi tyranny. When German soldiers entered the Warsaw ghetto on April 19, 1943, to round up Jews for a final deportation to death camps, only six thousand of the half-million people who had once crowded it remained alive. The Nazi soldiers had expected it would be easy to round up the weak, unarmed Jews. To their surprise, they were greeted by gunfire from about twelve hundred members of the Jewish Fighting Organization, a resistance group that had formed. Armed with pistols, homemade Molotov cocktails (bottles filled with gasoline), and two machine guns that had been smuggled into the ghetto, they fought fiercely, killing scores of Nazi soldiers and wounding many others.

Although outnumbered by heavily armed troops, the ghetto defenders in the next few days managed to beat back a second German advance. On April 23 Mordecai Anielewicz, the commander of the revolt, wrote a summary on the fighting in which he praised the resistance: "One thing is clear, what happened exceeded our boldest dreams. The Germans ran twice from the ghetto. . . . I feel that great things are happening and what we dared do is of great, enormous importance."[78]

Anielewicz was killed shortly after he wrote that message, and eventually almost all the Jews battling the Germans were killed as well. Although they managed to fight for almost a month and killed hundreds of Nazi soldiers, the outcome was never in doubt. In the end, the Germans defeated them by destroying the ghetto building by building and killing everyone they found.

CAMP REVOLTS

Even people who had already been transported to death camps sometimes managed to fight back. The first camp revolt came on August 2, 1943, in Treblinka

The Nazis route out Jews during the Warsaw ghetto uprising. Despite a valiant attempt to avoid deportation, Warsaw's Jews were ultimately defeated.

when some one thousand Jewish prisoners who had stolen axes and firearms from a supply area set fire to the camp and staged a mass escape. Although two hundred inmates managed to escape, about half were captured and killed.

Another camp revolt occurred on October 14, 1943, at the death camp Sobibor. Some six hundred prisoners rose up and killed eleven SS guards and police auxiliaries. The uprising was led by captured Soviet soldiers, including Alexander Pechersky, who was Jewish. They were armed with knives and hatchets that were made in an on-site iron factory. They also had several hand grenades, pistols, and a rifle stolen by some Jewish women who cleaned soldiers' quarters.

When guards came to inspect their living quarters, Sobibor prisoners killed several of them and began shouting "Hurrah!" the signal for the escape attempt. About three hundred prisoners were killed trying to escape, but the rest managed to get through the fences, barbed wire, and minefields surrounding the camp. Although more than two hundred escapees were later found and killed, fifty won their freedom. Pechersky described their experience as they left the camp behind: "Six hundred pain-racked, tormented people surged forward with a wild 'Hurrah' to life and freedom. And there we were on the other side of the fence and minefield. And running faster, faster through the barren strip of land."[79]

Another major prison rebellion occurred at Auschwitz on October 7, 1944. It was led by a *Sonderkommando* who had learned that all the inmates were going to be killed. The revolt began when *Sonderkommando* Chaim Neuhof struck an SS guard. The prisoners then attacked guards with a variety of tools, and cut holes in nearby fences through which they could flee to the forest that surrounded the camp. Salmen Lewental described how prisoners attacked guards (his notes survived because he buried them in a jar): "They showed an immense courage [and] hurled themselves upon the guards with hammers and axes, wounded some of them, the rest they beat with what they could get at, they pelted them with stones."[80]

Although about 250 prisoners broke out, they were all captured and killed. The Germans also murdered several hundred other prisoners as punishment for the revolt. Despite their limited success, the camp revolts are considered an example of how the human will to resist oppression cannot be completely broken, even by the most horrible conditions.

JEWISH FIGHTERS

Many prisoners who escaped camps or ghettos joined groups of armed civilians that were part of the resistance movement that existed in most countries Germany conquered. Members of such groups were called partisans. These small, mobile forces operated out of dense forest areas where the Germans had trouble finding them. They attacked military targets such as troop trains, ammunition dumps, and small groups of soldiers. One of the most famous acts of any resistance group occurred in Czechoslovakia on May 29, 1942, when three partisans killed Nazi leader Reinhard Heydrich by blowing up his car near Prague.

One Jewish fighter was Max Grosblat, who escaped from the Dubno ghetto in

Poland and joined a partisan group. "Not all the Jewish people went to death like sheep. Some of us were fighting,"[81] he said proudly years later. Grosblat earned the nickname "Fearless Mischa" [Mischa is a variation on Max] for his courage in fighting the Nazis. Said Grosblat, "We blew up bridges, and when German trains were going to the front with ammunition and weapons, we put dynamite under the tracks. You had to hide and pull a string to ignite it. Nobody wanted that job, so I did it."[82]

Some partisan groups were composed entirely of Jews. For example, four separate units with about four hundred fighters operated near Vilna, Lithuania. Celia K., a Jew who escaped from the Vilna ghetto, said living conditions for partisans were harsh: They lived in caves or the open forest, had to steal almost everything they ate, and were always in danger of being attacked by the Germans. Celia K. rode a horse on raids against soldiers and Lithuanians who helped the Nazis, saying, "We killed [them] mercilessly."[83]

JAN KARSKI, HOLOCAUST WITNESS

In 1942 Jan Karski, a member of a Polish resistance group, performed one of the most important tasks of the resistance when he risked his life to gather infor-

Lithuanian partisans like these were among the many Jewish fighters who resisted the Nazis during the war.

"THE TOMORROW DID NOT WORRY US"

Zivia Lubetkin was one of the resistance fighters who fought in the Warsaw ghetto uprising. To Lubetkin, it was a day of wonder to see Jews killing Germans instead of the other way around. Her comments on the victory during the first day of the battle are from Martin Gilbert's The Holocaust: A History of the Jews of Europe During the Second World War.

It was strange to see those twenty men and women, Jewish men and women, standing up against the armed great enemy glad and merry, because we knew that their end will come. We knew that they will conquer us first, but to know that for our lives they would pay a high price. When the Germans came up to our posts and marched by and we threw those hand grenades and bombs, and saw German blood pouring over the streets of Warsaw, after we saw so much Jewish blood running in the streets of Warsaw before that, there was rejoicing. The tomorrow did not worry us. The rejoicing amongst Jewish fighters was great and to see the wonder and the miracle, those German heroes retreated, afraid and terrorized from the Jewish bombs and hand grenades, home-made. . . . And thus on the first day, we the few with our poor arms drove the Germans away from the ghetto.

---

mation about the Holocaust. Karski, a Christian, first sneaked into the Warsaw ghetto and then into a small transit camp where Jews were robbed of their possessions before being sent to Belzec to be killed. Armed with facts he learned firsthand and reports from others about how Germans were killing Jews, Karski traveled to England and the United States to tell top leaders what was going on; in July 1943 he even met with President Franklin D. Roosevelt.

Karski's eyewitness account was the most detailed and moving report about the Holocaust that had come out of Europe at that point. But when the Allies said there was nothing they could do to stop the deaths, Karski believed he had failed in his mission to aid Jews. Decades later, Karski harshly criticized the decision to wait until the war ended to try and save victims:

> [My Catholic] faith tells me [a terrible mistake] has been committed by humanity: through commission, or omission, or self-imposed ignorance, or insensitivity, or self-interest, or hypocrisy, or heartless rationalization. This sin [not helping victims] will haunt humanity to the end of time.[84]

7 Holocaust Survivors Make New Lives

On April 11, 1945, U.S. soldiers liberated the Buchenwald concentration camp, freeing inmate Elie Wiesel from a brutal, degrading existence that reduced him to little more than a walking skeleton. So ill that he had to be hospitalized, Wiesel was unable to look at himself in a mirror for two weeks. In *Night*, Wiesel wrote that the image he saw would haunt him forever:

> One day I was able to get up, after gathering all my strength. I wanted to see myself in the mirror hanging on the opposite wall. I had not seen myself since the ghetto. From the depths of the mirror, a corpse gazed back at me. The look in his eyes, as they stared into mine, has never left me.[85]

Wiesel was sixteen years old in 1944 when his family was deported from Romania to concentration camps, where his parents and sister would die. His father, made ill by overwork and starvation, passed away while sleeping in the bunk below his son in January 1945. Despite the horror of his experiences, Wiesel, like other survivors, was able to make a new life for himself after World War II. It was one dedicated to educating the world about the Holocaust. His work would earn him many awards, including the prestigious 1986 Nobel Peace Prize. But Wiesel would never have been able to begin his new life if he had not been freed from the Nazis.

LIBERATING CONCENTRATION CAMPS

Allied soldiers began liberating concentration camps near the end of World War II. There were no battles for the concentration camps; German guards simply fled from advancing soldiers. The first camp freed was Majdanek in Poland. When Soviet soldiers entered it on July 23, 1944, they were shocked by what they saw. There were mountains of dead people and huge ovens with partially burned bodies. The one thousand surviving prisoners looked like living corpses. Entire buildings full of clothing and personal possessions hinted that thousands of other people had been murdered as well. In October when the *Illustrated London News* ran horrifying pictures of Majdanek, it said it was publishing them because "the enormity of the crimes perpetrated by the Germans is so wicked that our readers [may] think the reports of such crimes exaggerated or due to propaganda."[86]

Other newspapers also bore witness to the terrible crimes committed in the camps. For example, after U.S. soldiers liberated Buchenwald in April 1945, Marguerite Higgins of the *New York Herald Tribune* filed a story about two young brothers she found wandering in the camp. When Higgins asked where their parents were, one of the boys replied, "All the older people were burned up."[87]

Despite the graphic photos and stories, the world had trouble accepting the horrible truth. Even American soldiers hardened by war were shocked by what they saw, especially the stick-thin figures with haunted faces who tottered forward or crawled to joyously greet them. "It looked like the land of the living dead. They were nothing but walking skeletons,"[88] said William McBurney, a soldier whose battalion liberated prisoners.

Many soldiers were so horrified by starving inmates in their tattered prison uniforms that they broke down and wept while handing out candy bars and other food they had. One American soldier who helped free Gunskirchen camp near Lambach, Austria, was especially overwhelmed by what he found. Major Cameron Coffman explains:

An unforgettable drama was enacted when a sergeant of our group of five raced out of one building, his face

Inmates cheer as Allied soldiers liberate their camp. Liberation of the concentration camps began in 1944 as the Allies retook German-controlled areas.

DEATH MARCH

Judy Cohen was forced to embark on a death march in April 1945. She was freed by American soldiers on May 5, 1945, on a road near a small German town called Düben. Fewer than two hundred of the initial five hundred prisoners, survived the march. In a personal reflection posted on the Internet, Cohen recalled her experience.

I have no idea how long this march lasted. Maybe twelve days or maybe less. We had no calendar. All I know is that we marched and starved, starved and marched for there was no supply of anything for us . . . . I have no idea how [two friends] and I managed to survive. We lived and acted like animals. Raiding garbage cans, begging, ate rotten vegetables dug from the fields. I remember an overwhelming desire to eat and not move my body—ever again. Just eat and rest and get rid of the lice covering my clothes and body. Those were my very modest wishes. As the days wore on, my feet were bloodier and bloodier, for all I had was wooden clogs held together by a piece of canvas and a piece of cord. Those who couldn't keep up were left by the wayside to die. We were not the only "marchers" on the roads in Nazi Germany. Every day we saw "marchers" like ourselves, in striped clothing, dragging themselves on the other side of the road, going in opposite directions. There was this unbelievable, no-rhyme-or-reason, marching during the last few weeks before the end of the war and the Holocaust.

flaming with rage. The sergeant, a Jewish boy of Polish descent, had found three of his relatives lying in the filth of that barracks. They are sleeping tonight between white sheets for the first time in three years in one of the better homes in Lambach.[89]

FIRST MOMENTS OF FREEDOM

For inmates like David Yeager, a Polish Jew imprisoned in Buchenwald, the soldiers who freed them from their hellish existence seemed like they had come from another world. Said Yeager:

I thought they had come down from heaven [and] I thought I must be hallucinating. I grabbed one of the soldiers by the arm and kissed him. "Are you American?" I asked him over and over. He was crying. I couldn't because by then I had no life left in me, not even enough for crying.[90]

Not all prisoners were in camps when they were freed. Judy Cohen was liberated near Düben, Germany, when U.S. soldiers chased away Nazis guarding her and other Jews. She was one of fewer than two hundred survivors of a death march of two thousand inmates. "The joy of liberation!" Cohen later recalled. "We comprehended its significance only in terms of that moment's misery—what it will do for our bodily needs [especially to] eat and eat and eat, knowing that tomorrow we can eat again. To be free of fear!"[91]

The soldiers soon began feeding prisoners who had endured overwhelming hunger for so long. But in a cruel twist of fate, many became sick or died from eating because their bodies were no longer accustomed to such rich fare. Said Sarah Friedmann, who was freed on April 29, 1945, near Allach, Germany: "Many perished that day as a result of overeating such fat and nourishing food. We called them 'canned goods' victims."[92]

In fact, food and liberation could not help many prisoners. For weeks after the liberations, hundreds of inmates, some of them weighing only sixty pounds, died from starvation and illness despite the efforts of military doctors to save them. The initial excitement of being liberated also led to death for some prisoners. At Dachau, at least three people died when they accidentally touched electrified fences as they rushed to greet soldiers.

In the liberated camps, the hatred inmates felt for their former captors sometimes gave way to vengeance. Inmates beat or hanged some Nazi guards while Allied soldiers, believing justice was being done, calmly watched. Joseph K., a Polish Jew liberated from Flossenbürg, remembers how a U.S. soldier offered him the chance to kill Germans with a machine gun: "He handed it to me, motioning to kill the German prisoners. I became very frightened and I gave it back to him. I just walked away."[93]

"To Get Such a Greeting Was Devastating"

The initial exhilaration of having been freed faded for inmates as they began to think about what would happen next. As Judy Cohen said, "After we became 'born-again' human beings, the anguish set in. We started to think about the future. The question we all asked, I asked: 'What now?'"[94]

Some prisoners returned to their war-torn hometowns. Although Christians were received joyously, Jews were often greeted with hostility because so many Poles were anti-Semitic and still hated Jewish people. Henry Slamovich was one of two dozen Jews who in May 1945 went back to Dzialoszyce, Poland: "We thought to ourselves, 'We had survived. We are alive. We are going to enjoy our freedom,'"[95] Slamovich said. But within a week their former neighbors had murdered four of them, partly because they feared that returning Jews would seek the homes and possessions they had been forced to leave behind when the Nazis took them away. Slamovich and the others left after facing continuous hostile treatment. Said Slamovich: "It hurts more what the Poles did even than what the Germans did. After coming home, to get such a greeting was devastating."[96]

In the first year after the war ended, more than a thousand Jews were killed in Poland because of lingering anti-Semitism. The worst incident came on July 4, 1946, in Kielce when a savage mob murdered forty-two Jews and wounded another fifty. After the Kielce massacre, five thousand Jews fled Poland as they once had the Nazis.

Displaced Persons

The Jews who could not return to their homes in Poland were among several million people from countries throughout Europe who, after the war, had no place to live. Labeled displaced persons (DPs) by the Allies, they included Holocaust survivors as well as people from eastern European countries that had been taken over by the Soviet Union (many people did not want to live under Communist rule because it denied them personal freedom, so they fled their homes).

To temporarily care for the DPs, the Allies established camps in Germany, Austria, and Italy. The United Nations Relief and Rehabilitation Administration (UNRRA) administered the camps, some of which housed more than five thousand people. Initially they were overcrowded, dirty, and provided only the barest basic needs of shelter and food. To separate inhabitants from nearby civilian populations, they were surrounded by barbed-wire fences, making them look like Nazi concentration camps. After receiving complaints about the camps, President Harry S. Truman appointed Pennsylvania Law School dean Earl Harrison to investigate them. Harrison's report of his July 1945 visit to over thirty camps harshly criticized the conditions he found:

> We [the United States] appear to be treating the Jews as the Nazis treated them, except that we do not exterminate them. They are in concentration camps in large numbers under our military guard instead of [German] troops. One is led to wonder whether

the German people seeing this are not supposing that we are following or at least condoning Nazi policy.[97]

Harrison's report led to improvements in DP camps, including the removal of barbed wire. The UNRRA gave DPs better food, created schools to educate children and teach adults job skills, and provided more opportunities for religious and social activities. Because the largest single group of DPs were Jews—their population in the camps reached a high of 250,000 in 1947—Jewish groups in America began donating huge quantities of clothing, food, and other supplies.

The improved conditions allowed DPs to engage in a limited social life, including attending plays and concerts. Most survivors were young people, and many fell in love and married. As a result, from 1946 to 1948 the camps had the highest birth rate in the world.

Immigration

But the longer people were kept in the DP camps, the more they wanted to get out and start new lives somewhere else. They could not leave, however, until a country would accept them as immigrants. Although for several years few nations wanted to bear the burden of accepting so many new citizens, countries gradually began to welcome displaced persons and the camps began to empty.

The majority of DPs wanted to go to the United States because of its reputation for religious tolerance. Madeline Deutsch, who was sent to Auschwitz when she was fourteen, remembers the deep emotion she and other immigrants

Jewish DPs, or displaced persons, await transport to their new homes. Many DPs hoped to immigrate to America because of that country's reputation for religious tolerance.

felt upon their arrival: "Practically everybody I think bent down and kissed the good old American soil because this finally meant freedom. We were finally, after all these years, free."[98]

One of the grateful newcomers was Tom Lantos, a Jewish youth who had been placed in a work camp in 1944 when Germany invaded Hungary. In August 1947, the nineteen-year-old Lantos came to America to study at the University of Washington. Lantos not only graduated from college but became a U.S. citizen and in 1981 was elected to Congress. Lantos said he quickly realized the wonderful opportunities America offered him when he arrived in Seattle:

[Arriving in America was] totally unreal. Here I was, coming out of the Holocaust, starvation, poverty, persecution, the worst horror of mankind, and I had landed in this [charming] setting. People were friendly and wonderful, there was all the food I could eat. I couldn't believe my eyes.[99]

Another new American was John M. Komski, a Polish youth who survived five concentration camps including Auschwitz. After four years in DP camps in Germany, where he married another Auschwitz survivor, Komski was finally granted permission to immigrate to the United States. Komski was a Roman

"Haven't We Suffered Enough?"

Anti-Semitism persisted in Europe even after the war ended. In Gilbert's The Holocaust, *Holocaust survivor Ben Helfgott describes how he and his cousin were arrested when they tried to return home to Poland.*

The two officers menacingly extracted the pistols from their holsters, and ordered us to walk to the nearest wall. I emitted a torrent of desperate appeals and entreaties. I pleaded with them, "Haven't we suffered enough? Haven't the Nazis caused enough destruction and devastation to all of us [Jews and Poles alike]? Our common enemy is destroyed and the future is ours. We have survived against all odds and why are you intent on promoting the heinous crimes that the Nazis have unleashed?" . . . I went on in the same vein speaking agitatedly for some time. Eventually, one of the officers succumbed to my pleas and said, "Let's leave them, they are after all still boys." As they put away their pistols, they made a remark which still rings loud in my ears. "You can consider yourselves very lucky. We have killed many of your kind. You are the first ones we have left alive." With this comment they disappeared into the dark of the night.

Catholic, a religious group that made up over half of the DPs who came to America until 1952, the year the camps closed.

Establishing Israel

While many Jews immigrated to America, many others went to the Middle East, where they hoped to establish a Jewish homeland. According to the Bible, Jewish people originally lived in Israel, a narrow strip of land on the eastern shore of the Mediterranean Sea. By A.D. 135 the Romans had conquered Israel, renamed it Palestine, and forced most Jews to leave. Palestine was later conquered by the Muslim Ottoman Empire, which ruled it for hundreds of years. At the end of World War I, the new League of Nations gave Great Britain the right to govern it.

Even though Palestine was ruled for centuries by other nations, Jewish people still considered it their historic homeland. In the late 1800s, a movement called Zionism began among European Jews; its goal was to establish a Jewish homeland in Palestine where Jews would be safe from anti-Semitism. After World War II, the desire to create a Jewish homeland grew stronger than ever. When American journalist I.F. Stone visited the DP camps, he heard one plea over and over: "I am a Jew. That's enough. We have wandered enough. We have worked and struggled too long on the lands of other people. We must build a land of our own."[100]

When Great Britain began restricting Jewish immigrants from Palestine, Jewish groups illegally smuggled an estimated forty thousand DPs into the area. The groups also tried to have Jews sail to Palestine, but the British captured almost every ship and sent passengers back to Europe or interred them on the island of Cyprus. After the voyage of one ship from Europe called the *Exodus* was stopped in July 1947, the ship's forty-five hundred passengers went on a hunger strike to protest not being allowed to go to Palestine. When the ship finally docked at a German port, British soldiers had to forcibly remove passengers.

News stories about the incident, including photographs of the brutal way Holocaust survivors were taken off the ship, helped turn world opinion against the British. After much deliberation and controversy, Great Britain agreed to give up control of portions of Palestine to the Jews.

On May 14, 1948, Jewish leaders declared the new state of Israel. When the new nation opened its borders to anyone who was Jewish, the remaining refugees in DP camps quickly emigrated there. One such person was Leah Silverstein, a native of Warsaw, Poland, who during World War II fought with resistance groups. Silverstein remembers her emotions when she arrived in the new Jewish homeland: "I was so happy to be there . . . finally the dream came true. I remember walking in the streets of Tel Aviv [its capital] and seeing inscriptions in the Hebrew language. My goodness, it was like a dream."[101]

LOOKING FOR LOVED ONES

Even after starting their new lives, survivors could not forget the horrors they had endured in the Holocaust. One of the most anguishing things was not

Jews await the proper documents to allow them to travel to Israel.

knowing if family members and friends had survived. Chaotic postwar conditions made it difficult for survivors to find each other. Some people located loved ones by reviewing lists of DP camp residents or discovered they had died by reading lists of victims compiled from official concentration camp records.

Many survivors also searched for loved ones on their own. For example, when Pol-ish Jew Max Schwartz was freed from Buchenwald, he tried to locate his brother. Schwartz at first could not find him, but he finally got a lead when he met some people on a train. Explains Schwartz, "I started to look if my brother is alive, stopping in every city and every town to ask. Then in a train was three or four people and we were talking, and one said, 'I know Abraham Schwartz. He is living not far from this town.' And he gave me the address for my brother!"[102] All too often, however, such searches ended in disappointment. People discovered that their loved ones had died or could find nothing conclusive on their fate.

Sometimes, it took people decades to accept the bitter truth about their relatives, as was the case with survivor Jeannine Burk. After the war, she was told her father had died at Auschwitz. Burk, however, never fully accepted this news and often fantasized that her father would one day come to see her. His death finally became real to her in 1986 when she came across records of Jews who had been deported by the Germans: "They had my father's name. There was the date taken but there was no date set free. I realized my father really was dead. But I was a grown woman. Imagine? All that time. That was the first time that I really said, 'Okay, my fa-

Jewish DPs display their new national flag from a train destined for Israel.

A New Life in America

Roman Ferber was twelve years old in 1945 when Soviet troops freed the young Polish Jew from the Auschwitz concentration camp. Five years later Ferber moved to America, where he created a whole new life for himself. Despite his accomplishments, Ferber never forgot what he suffered in the Holocaust. He explains in Elinor J. Brecher's Schindler's Legacy.

I am stuck with it [his memory of the experience], obviously. There is no way in the world you can forget. There is no way to describe visually, on film or anything else, what we went through, each one of us in a different way. When you see little babies being taken and thrown into [open pits], does that leave you with something for the rest of your life? Of course! I have forgiven, but I cannot forget. [Out] of nowhere, you get dreams, and when you get up in the morning and you look at your hands, it [a concentration camp tattoo] is there.

ther is dead and they did this. They did this.'"[103]

HOLOCAUST LEGACY

For survivors, the legacy of the Holocaust went beyond the loss of loved ones. Many suffered health and emotional problems for the rest of their lives because of what they endured in concentration camps. For example, Anna W., a Gypsy, was operated on at Ravensbrück by doctors experimenting with ways to sterilize women so that they could not become pregnant. Anna later married but could not have children. For her, therefore, the victims of the Holocaust included the children she was never able to have. In an interview decades later, Anna was asked if the operation still affected her life: "Very much, yes. For now I have to suffer from it. . . . I could have had a family, I could have had grandchildren who would be twenty years [old] by now, my grandchildren."[104]

Chapter

8 Bringing Nazi War Criminals to Justice

In the early morning hours of April 30, 1945, Nazi dictator Adolf Hitler committed suicide by shooting himself in the head as Soviet troops made their way toward his heavily guarded underground complex in Berlin. Although Hitler had often condemned suicide as cowardly, he killed himself in the final days of World War II because he could not endure the personal disgrace of losing a war he had started.

Hitler's death denied the world the opportunity to bring to justice the one man most responsible for the murder of 11 million people in the Holocaust, including nearly 6 million Jews. However, Allied soldiers quickly arrested other high-ranking Nazi leaders such as Hermann Göring, the second most powerful official after Hitler. Göring and thousands of other people who had conducted the twentieth century's most barbaric event would now have to stand trial for their crimes.

POSTWAR JUSTICE

Allied leaders had begun planning how to deal with Nazi officials and soldiers even before Germany surrendered. On November 1, 1943, representatives of the United States, Great Britain, and the Soviet Union signed a pact stating that they would charge and try Nazis for conducting the Holocaust and starting a conflict that caused the deaths of tens of millions of other people worldwide in the global combat of World War II.

The postwar trials the leaders authorized were historically unique. In the past, officials of defeated nations had rarely been prosecuted for what they did during a war. But in his opening statement at the first trial on November 21, 1945, American prosecutor Robert H. Jackson explained that the unusual legal proceedings were necessary because of the magnitude of the crimes committed. Jackson said that the Nazis needed to be punished as a warning to future leaders to never again do such terrible things: "The wrongs which we seek to condemn and punish have been so calculated, so malignant, and so devastating that civilization cannot tolerate their being ignored because it cannot survive their being repeated."[105]

Jackson's remarks opened the major war criminals trial, the first of thirteen held in Nuremberg, Germany, from 1945 to 1949. They are known collectively as the Nuremberg Trials because they were conducted at Nuremberg's Palace of Justice. The trials were held there because it was one of the few large German courtrooms that had not been destroyed during the war and because the city itself was a symbol of Nazi inhumanity. It was in Nuremberg that the Nazis in 1935 issued laws that stripped Jews of their rights as citizens, the first step in the Holocaust.

More than five thousand Nazi criminals were convicted between 1945 and 1949 in hundreds of trials, but the Nuremberg judicial proceedings were the most famous. The Nuremberg defendants included two hundred of the highest-ranking and best-known Nazis. The trials were conducted by the International Military Tribunal (IMT), which was made up of judges and prosecutors from France, Great Britain, the United States, and the Soviet Union.

THE HOLOCAUST ON TRIAL

The first Nuremberg trial captured the world's attention because the twenty-two defendants were well-known figures, including Göring; Hans Frank, the civilian leader in Poland who sent several million people to their deaths in concentration camps; Albert Speer, who directed arms production and other military industries; and Admiral Karl Dönitz, whom Hitler named his successor when he committed suicide. The charges against them and the defendants in other trials were split into three categories: crimes against peace, dealing with how they initiated World War II; war crimes, actions that violated international law during war, such as murdering captured soldiers; and crimes against

American attorney Robert H. Jackson prosecuted the first war criminals trial in Nuremberg, Germany in 1945.

SAVING EVIDENCE

In Martin Gilbert's Never Again: A History of the Holocaust, *war crimes investigator Benjamin B. Ferencz remembers how an inmate from Mauthausen concentration camp risked his life to save evidence that would help identify guards who had worked at the camp.*

An inmate embraced me joyfully. One of his jobs had been to type identification cards for the guards; when the guards were reassigned, the cards [were] to be destroyed. The inmate, whose name I shall never know, had at great risk to his life, failed to burn the cards. Instead he had buried them carefully in a field. After he greeted me he left the barrack and, a few minutes later, returned, unwrapped a soiled box, and handed me a complete record and picture of every man who had ever [worked] in the camp! It was invaluable evidence for a war crimes prosecutor. I was moved by the blind faith which inspired the unknown prisoner to risk his life in the conviction that there would come a day of reckoning.

humanity, which encompassed the murder of millions of people in the Holocaust and other inhumane acts against civilians, such as deporting them for slave labor.

The Holocaust was a key issue of the long, exhausting trial that began on November 20, 1945, and lasted 315 days. Much of the evidence came from 100,000 German documents ranging from concentration camp records to the diary of Nazi official Hans Frank, who was nicknamed the "Butcher of the Poles." One of his diary entries read, "The Jews must be eliminated. Whenever we catch one, it is his end."[106]

Prosecutors also introduced graphic photographs and films of liberated camps as well as dramatic survivor testimony. Jackson once told those assembled in the courtroom that much of what he presented was so grisly that "you will say I have robbed you of your sleep."[107] Some of the most horrifying testimony came from Marie Claude Vaillant-Couturier, a member of the French Resistance who endured three years at Auschwitz. On January 28, 1946, she testified about screams she heard there in 1942: "One night we were awakened by terrifying cries. And we discovered . . . that on the preceding day, the gas supply having run out, they had thrown the children into the furnaces alive."[108]

In the face of the overwhelming evidence against them, several defendants tried to claim that they had no direct knowledge of the Holocaust. For example, when questioned about German concentration camps, German foreign minister Joachim von Ribbentrop answered, "I knew nothing about that."[109] Ribbentrop's statement, however, appeared to be false.

A prosecutor produced a map showing that concentration camps were located near several of the Nazi leader's many homes; thus, it was highly unlikely that he was completely unaware of them.

After about eight months of testimony, on July 26, 1946, Jackson summed up the prosecution's case against the defendants. In a long, impassioned speech, Jackson not only reviewed the evidence against the Nazi officials but tried to put the enormity of the evil they had caused into historical perspective. Claimed Jackson:

These deeds are the overshadowing historical facts by which generations to come will remember this [century]. If we cannot eliminate the causes and

Nazi defendants await trial at Nuremberg. During their trials, some Nazi officials claimed to be unaware of the Holocaust despite the overwhelming evidence against them.

prevent the repetition of these barbaric events, it is not an irresponsible prophecy to say that this twentieth century may yet succeed in bringing the doom of civilization.[110]

On October 1, 1946, the IMT found eighteen of the twenty-two defendants guilty. It sentenced Göring and ten others to death by hanging and the rest to prison terms ranging from fifteen years to life. Göring escaped what he believed was a demeaning form of execution by swallowing a cyanide capsule that was smuggled into his prison cell. Frank and the others, however, were hanged on October 16.

OTHER NUREMBERG TRIALS

Several of the other Nuremberg Trials grouped defendants into categories based on the crimes with which they were charged. One trial included doctors who performed medical experiments in labor camps or killed people in the Nazi euthanasia program. In another proceeding, the defendants were judges who had used their legal authority to commit or permit war crimes. In yet another trial, twenty-four members of the *Einsatzgruppen* mass murder squads were prosecuted for killing more than 1 million innocent victims.

Chilling testimony by survivors once again played a key part in these legal proceedings. In the doctors' trial, Polish priest Leo Miechalowski explained how he was forced to undergo medical experiments at Dachau. The priest testified that he was first infected with malaria, which nearly killed him, and later subjected to cold-water immersion tests to find out how the human body responds to freezing temperatures. Miechalowski recalls the agonizing physical sensations he ex-

MEETING A NAZI WAR CRIMINAL

Sigmund Boraks is a Polish Jew who survived ghettos, labor camps, and concentration camps like Auschwitz and Dachau. In an interview with Tulane University, he recounts a chance meeting he had with a former Nazi.

After the war I was living in Germany and I was talking with a guy. He didn't know I was Jewish. Never asked. Never told him. One day it was Yom Kippur [a Jewish holiday] and I didn't come in [to work]. And he asked me, "You are Jew?" Like I'm a sick man. "Yes." He left me standing there. Later, about four weeks, he told me, "I was Einsatzgruppen. And I kill many women and children." He shot them. "This was the law." He had to follow the law. "They told me to do it," and he did it. I said, "How can you sleep at night?" I can understand soldier kill another soldier but civilian people? This was a war about civilian people more than anything else.

perienced when two guards threw him into a large tub of icy water: "All of a sudden I became very cold, and I began to tremble. I immediately turned to those two men and asked them to pull me out of the water because I would be unable to stand it much longer. However, they told me laughingly, 'Well, this will only last a very short time.'"[111] After an hour and a half, the priest finally lost consciousness.

Sixteen of the twenty-three physicians on trial were found guilty for such cruel experiments, and seven were sentenced to death. In addition to sentencing the doctors, the judges also acted to prevent such medical experiments from taking place in the future. The judges authored the ten-point Nuremberg Code, which forcefully outlines the rights people have regarding medical experiments. The code was universally accepted and today still helps protect people around the world from being forced to become human test subjects against their will.

In the *Einsatzgruppen* trial, many of the defendants said they were innocent of murder because they were simply following orders from their superiors. An example of this defense occurred on January 3, 1946, when General Otto Ohlendorf, who commanded *Einsatzgruppe D*, explained that he had no choice but to follow orders, even orders he had reservations about because he knew they were morally wrong. This is how his lawyer, Ludwig Babel, questioned him:

Babel: But did you have no scruples in regard to the execution of these orders?

Ohlendorf: Yes, of course.

Babel: And how is it that they were carried out regardless of these scruples?

Ohlendorf: Because to me it is inconceivable that a subordinate leader should not carry out orders given by the leaders of the state.[112]

That defense was rejected by IMT judges. They stated that no soldier or civilian official should ever follow orders requiring them to commit a crime or violate internationally accepted codes of conduct during time of war, such as how to treat POWs. That ethical standard is still used today to determine how soldiers should act during wartime.

SOME NAZIS ESCAPED

Although thousands of Nazis were tried for their crimes at the end of World War II, many more eluded capture. This was due to the chaotic postwar conditions that engulfed Europe, and also to concerted attempts to escape.

After it became apparent that Germany was going to lose the war, in 1944, a group of Nazi industrialists and bankers met with members of the SS to plan out how to help top civilian leaders and military officers avoid being captured. The group they formed, which became known as ODESSA, helped Nazis charged with war crimes assume new identities in Germany or travel to other countries. ODESSA was financed through contributions from the businessmen and secret funds Nazi officials had accumulated by selling Holocaust victims' valuable possessions, such as gold, jewels, and works of art.

Holocaust survivor Simon Wiesenthal spent his life after the war hunting Nazis who had escaped capture.

This secret organization was discovered by the War Crimes Section of the U.S. Army, which was established to document war crimes and track down individuals charged with such crimes. One of the investigators who revealed ODESSA to the world was Simon Wiesenthal, a Ukrainian Jew who was liberated from the Mauthausen concentration camp. Wiesenthal, who would spend the rest of his life hunting Nazis, explains how war criminals were able to begin new lives in other countries:

> We knew from several cases that they evidently had no difficulty in obtaining forged [identity] documents. Nor did they seem to have any problems about establishing a new livelihood: the top-ranking ones, at least, immediately had substantial financial resources at their disposal [to start businesses] and, if necessary, to bribe the authorities.[113]

THE CAPTURE OF A "MONSTER"

South America was a favored destination for escaped Nazis. For years after the war there were rumors that important war criminals such as Josef Mengele were living in Argentina and other nearby countries. One of the Nazis that ODESSA helped relocate to South America was SS lieutenant colonel Adolf Eichmann, who during the war worked out train schedules and other details to deport millions of Jews to their death in concentration camps. Although Allied officials searched for him after the war, Eichmann escaped to Argentina. He hid there successfully until 1959 when

Wiesenthal, in his continuing quest to hunt down Nazis, read a story in an Austrian newspaper about the death of Eichmann's stepmother. Listed as a survivor was Vera Eichmann, the Nazi's wife. Wiesenthal did some investigating and found out that she was living in Buenos Aires, Argentina, and was reportedly married to a man named Ricardo Klement.

Suspecting that Klement might be Eichmann, Wiesenthal contacted officials in Israel, who sent secret service agents to Argentina. They discovered that Klement

EICHMANN TRIAL LEGACY

Simon Wiesenthal helped track down Adolf Eichmann so he could be tried and sentenced for his role in the Holocaust. In his book Justice Not Vengeance, *Wiesenthal explains the great benefit of Eichmann's capture and trial.*

What then was the real success of the hunting down of Eichmann! It reminded the world of the tragedy of the Jews at the time [1960] when it seemed to be being repressed and forgotten. After the Eichmann trial, no one could doubt any longer the extent of the tragedy. It was Eichmann's evidence that destroyed the fairy tale that Auschwitz was just a lie. The Eichmann trial, moreover, substantially enhanced our knowledge of the Nazi murder machinery and its principal operators. [It also taught the world] that fanatical, near-pathological sadism is not necessary for millions of people to be murdered; that all that is needed is dutiful obedience to some "leader."

Adolf Eichmann appears in court after his capture in 1960.

was indeed Eichmann. The Israeli agents then worked out an elaborate plan to arrest him and take him to Israel for trial. They abducted Eichmann on May 11, 1960, when he stepped off a bus. Nine days later the agents flew him to Israel, completing the most daring capture ever of a former Nazi official.

Convicted in 2004, Ladislav Niznansky (pictured) was one of the last Nazis tried. The United Nations and the United States continue to hunt Nazis who evaded capture.

Eichmann's trial in Israel was the first one shown on television, and it was broadcast around the world. Even though Eichmann claimed "I am not the monster that I am made out to be,"[114] millions of people who watched the trial disagreed. Seated in a bullet-proof glass booth because authorities feared someone would try to kill him, for sixteen weeks Eichmann faced testimony from more than one hundred witnesses, many of them Holocaust survivors. Witnesses and documents detailed the role Eichmann had played in transporting millions of Jews to the concentration camps.

After months of dramatic testimony, Eichmann was found guilty on fifteen separate charges. He then made a plea for mercy in which he claimed he had never wanted to kill anyone: "It was not my wish to slay people. The guilt for the mass murder is solely that of the political leaders."[115] The Israeli court rejected his attempt to exonerate himself from the millions of lives he had helped take and condemned Eichmann to death. He was hanged on May 31, 1962.

THE NAZI HUNT CONTINUES

Many nations have continued to find, try, and convict Nazis whose names appeared on lists prepared by the United Nations War Crimes Commission at the end of World War II. The search for war criminals has dragged on for decades because finding them has been very difficult.

Many prison guards and low-level officials avoided capture by the Allies after the war because they were not as well known as top Nazi figures like Eichmann and thus not recognized by officials looking for war criminals. It was also very difficult to identify Nazis in the postwar period because so many military and civilian records had been destroyed in the fighting and because so many Nazis lied about their past. In these ways, many Nazis were allowed to legally immigrate to other countries. For example, it is believed that as many as ten thousand people who were classified as war criminals or had Nazi connections came to the United States. Most entered the country without being identified as criminals because there was no evidence revealing them as Nazis. "They came through the front door with their papers [immigration forms] in order,"[116] said Alan Ryan, former director of the U.S. Justice Department's Office of Special Investigations (OSI).

OSI is the agency Congress authorized in 1979 to hunt down war criminals. OSI has sought evidence to identify former Nazis who have immigrated to America and illegally obtained citizenship. Since 1979 it has stripped 71 former Nazis of U.S. citizenship and deported 57 of them. OSI has also used the information to stop more than 160 other suspected Nazis from entering America.

The effort to bring Nazis to justice worldwide has continued into the twenty-first century. In April 2004, three former SS officers in Germany were tried and found guilty of slaughtering 560 people in the Italian village of Sant' Anna di Stazzema on August 12, 1944. And in the United States on April 30, 2004, the Justice Department won a decision in federal appeals court to strip Ukrainian John Demjanjuk, an eighty-four-year-old Cleveland, Ohio, resident, of his citizenship. The federal government claims that he was a guard in five concentration camps, including Sobibor, and it has been trying to deport him for over a decade. OSI director Eli Rosenbaum says the Demjanjuk decision is important because "[it] sends a powerful message to every participant in this ghastly Nazi campaign of genocide who is still living in this country: The government will not waver in its determination to find you, prosecute you, and remove you from the United States."[117]

An Eternal Guilt

Even after the Nazis responsible for the Holocaust have all died, what they did will live forever in the annals of history. Hans Frank admitted as much during his trial on April 18, 1946, when he accepted responsibility for the deaths of millions of people and acknowledged the terrible legacy of the Holocaust. Said Frank, "A thousand years will pass and this guilt of Germany will not be erased."[118]

Remembering the Holocaust

When Adolf Hitler came to power in Germany, he boasted that the Nazi regime he had named the Third Reich would last a thousand years. Although the Allies' victory in World War II snuffed out Hitler's fledgling empire after just twelve years and four months, historian William L. Shirer claims, "In that flicker of time, as history goes, it caused an eruption on this earth more violent and shattering than any previously experienced."[119]

The legacy Hitler left behind was one of horror—the murder of 11 million people, the shattered lives of Holocaust survivors, and the physical ruin of much of Europe. Yet survivors and many other people believe it is important that the world never forget such tragedy. In his March 2000 visit to a Holocaust memorial site in Israel, Pope John Paul II explained why this is necessary:

> More than half a century has passed [since the Holocaust], but the memories remain. No one can forget or ignore what happened. No one can diminish its scale. We wish to remember. But we wish to remember for a purpose, namely to ensure that never again will evil prevail, as it did for the millions of innocent victims of Nazism.[120]

THE NEED TO SHARE

For the physically and emotionally scarred survivors who emerged from concentration camps, hiding places, or the ranks of resistance groups at the end of World War II, the memories of the Holocaust were a burden they would carry all their lives. Many had an urgent need to share their pain after they were freed.

Primo Levi, an Italian Jew who survived Auschwitz, felt compelled to write about the Holocaust because he was afraid that his experiences would be forgotten or ignored: "I felt such an overpowering need to talk about it that [at first] I talked out loud. Later I chose to write it as the equivalent of talking about it. . . . The intention to 'leave an eyewitness account' came later, the primary need was to write for purposes of liberation [of his own emotions]."[121] Other survivors felt this same need to write or speak publicly about their experiences.

John M. Komski, a Polish Catholic who was in five concentration camps including Auschwitz, expressed himself in a different way. After immigrating to America, he worked as an artist for the *Washington Post* newspaper and painted critically acclaimed pictures of concentration camp life. Komski once explained why he needed to resurrect the bitter images of his past: "The reason I am doing these paintings is because I always thought it only destiny or providence that

allowed me to live when I knew there were tens of thousands of people who died [in concentration camps]. I wanted to do something to show the misery."[122]

LEST THE WORLD FORGET

Not all survivors felt comfortable sharing their experiences in this way, however. After immigrating to New Orleans, Louisiana, in 1950, Auschwitz survivor Dora Niederman never wanted to discuss what had happened to her during

A crowd gathers at the opening of the United States Holocaust Memorial Museum in Washington D.C.

the Holocaust. "For many years I didn't discuss the past. None of us did. It was painful for us to talk about it,"[123] she said.

Her attitude changed in 1989 when a racist named David Duke won a seat in the Louisiana State Legislature and then ran for other offices like the U.S. Senate. Duke was a Holocaust denier, a person who claims it never occurred or that the number of people killed was quite small. Inspired to defend her past, Niederman, and other survivors, began speaking to students in schools to counter such lies. "Duke kept on hollering on TV, 'Not such a thing as the Holocaust. It's a hoax. It's not true,'" says Niederman. "So all of us who live here in New Orleans come out and talk about it. We were there. We suffered for being Jewish."[124]

In addition to making sure the world continues to remember the Holocaust, survivors like Simon Wiesenthal believe that people need to understand the hatred that fueled it. In *Justice Not Vengeance*, Wiesenthal explains that there are many people all over the world who are still persecuted for their beliefs or race and understanding the Holocaust can help avert another disaster of that magnitude:

> It worries me that young people—particularly in the United States—may believe that the Third Reich could never repeat itself. Least of all in their own country. That is not so: hatred can be nurtured anywhere [and] unless we are vigilant, the history of the [future] will read like this: the beast in human shape got hold of a machine gun and, for the first time, was able to exterminate anything that moved.[125]

AN IMPORTANT LESSON

In order to stop future Holocausts, however, people have to be willing to defend the rights of those who are persecuted, regardless of their race, religion, gender, nationality, or ethnicity. This lesson was summed up by Reverend Martin Niemöller, a German Lutheran minister who survived incarceration in several concentration camps. Niemöller claimed the Holocaust was allowed to happen because people had lacked the courage to stand up for victims when the Nazis began sending them to concentration camps. Said Niemöller:

> First they came for the socialists, and I did not speak out—because I was not a socialist. Then they came for the trade unionists, and I did not speak out—because I was not a trade unionist. Then they came for the Jews, and I did not speak out—because I was not a Jew. Then they came for me—and there was no one left to speak for me.[126]

His powerful words are a reminder that when a government discriminates against one type of person, everyone's rights are in jeopardy. If they do not speak out against persecution, they may be among the next group to lose their rights, their freedom, and even their lives. It was a lack of courage to stand up to the Nazis that allowed the Holocaust to happen. And the guilt for this failure is shared by both German citizens and government officials in other countries such as the United States who did nothing to stop it.

Notes

Introduction:
A Twentieth-Century Horror

1. Quoted in Robert S. Wistrich, *Hitler and the Holocaust*. New York: Modern Library, 2001, p. 211.

2. Quoted in Otto Friedrich, *The Kingdom of Auschwitz*. New York: HarperCollins, 1994, p. 102.

Chapter 1: The Seeds of the Holocaust

3. Quoted in Eve Nussbaum Soumerai and Carol D. Schulz, *Daily Life During the Holocaust*. Westport, CT: Greenwood, 1998, p. 22.

4. Quoted in William L. Shirer, *The Rise and Fall of the Third Reich: A History of Nazi Germany*. New York: Simon & Schuster, 1960, p. 31.

5. Quoted in Shirer, *The Rise and Fall of the Third Reich*, p. 31.

6. Adolf Hitler, *Mein Kampf*. Boston: Houghton Mifflin, 1971, p. 22.

7. Hitler, *Mein Kampf*, p. 135.

8. Quoted in Wistrich, *Hitler and the Holocaust*, p. 39.

9. Hitler, *Mein Kampf*, pp. 496–97.

10. Quoted in Soumerai and Schulz, *Daily Life During the Holocaust*, p. 22.

11. Quoted in Alan Bullock, *Hitler: A Study in Tyranny*. New York: Smithmark, 1995, p. 107.

Chapter 2:
The Nazis Strip People of Their Rights

12. Hitler, *Mein Kampf*, p. 450.

13. Quoted in Louis L. Snyder, *Encyclopedia of the Third Reich*. New York: McGraw-Hill, 1976, p. 286.

14. Shirer, *The Rise and Fall of the Third Reich*, p. 192.

15. Quoted in Lucy S. Dawidowicz, *The War Against the Jews 1933–1945*. New York: Holt, Rinehart, and Winston, 1975, p. 52.

16. Quoted in Michael Burleigh, *The Third Reich: A New History*. New York: Hill & Wang, 2000, p. 283.

17. Quoted in Burleigh, *The Third Reich*, p. 112.

18. Quoted in Wistrich, *Hitler and the Holocaust*, p. 64.

19. Quoted in Rhoda G. Lewin, ed., *Witnesses to the Holocaust: An Oral History*. Boston: Twayne, 1990, p. 9.

20. Quoted in Martin Gilbert, *The Holocaust: A History of the Jews of Europe During the Second World War*. New York: Henry Holt, 1985, p. 69.

21. Quoted in Gilbert, *The Holocaust*, p. 74.

22. Quoted in Gunter Grau, *Hidden Holocaust? Gay and Lesbian Persecution in Germany 1933–45*. New York: Villiers House, 1995, p. 25.

23. Quoted in Soumerai and Schulz, *Daily Life During the Holocaust*, p. 45.

24. Quoted in Michael Berenbaum, *The World Must Know: The History of the Holocaust as Told in the United States Holocaust Memorial Museum*. Boston: Little, Brown, 1993, p. 64.

25. Berenbaum, *The World Must Know*, p. 65.

Chapter 3: Life in Jewish Ghettos

26. Quoted in William L. Shulman, "Anatomy of a Ghetto," Holocaust Resource Center and Archives, www.qcc.cuny.edu/HRCA/news/anatomy_of_ghetto_p1.htm.

27. Quoted in Soumerai and Schulz, *Daily Life During the Holocaust*, p. 105.

28. Quoted in Michael E. Stevens, ed., *Voices of the Wisconsin Past: Remembering the Holocaust*. Madison: State Historical Society of Wisconsin, 1997, p. 125.

29. Quoted in Lewin, *Witnesses to the Holocaust*, p. 51.

30. Quoted in Dawidowicz, *The War Against the Jews*, p. 203.

31. Quoted in Wolfgang Benz, *The Holocaust: A German Historian Examines the Genocide*. New York: Columbia University Press, 1999, p. 54.

32. Quoted in Stevens, *Voices of the Wisconsin Past*, p. 118.

33. Quoted in Lewin, *Witnesses to the Holocaust*, p. 28.

34. Quoted in Michael Grynberg, ed., *Words to Outlive Us: Eyewitness Accounts from the Warsaw Ghetto*. New York: Henry Holt, 2002, p. 38.

35. Quoted in Solon Beinfeld, "The Cultural Life of the Vilna Ghetto," Simon Wiesenthal Center, 1997. http://motlc.wiesenthal.org/resources/books/annual1/chap01.html.

36. Quoted in Emanuel Ringelblum, "Life in the Warsaw Ghetto," A Teacher's Guide to the Holocaust, 2001. http://fcit.coedu.usf.edu/holocaust/resource/document/DocRing1.htm.

37. Quoted in Martin Gilbert, *Never Again: A History of the Holocaust*. New York: Universe, 2002, p. 59.

38. Quoted in Lewin, *Witnesses to the Holocaust*, p. 96.

39. Louisiana Holocaust Survivors, "Anne Levy," www.tulane.edu/~so-inst/levy.html.

40. Quoted in Benz, *The Holocaust*, p. 49.

41. Quoted in Berenbaum, *The World Must Know*, p. 82.

Chapter 4:
The Final Solution: Mass Killing Begins

42. Quoted in Deborah Dwork and Robert Jan van Pelt, *Holocaust: A History*. New York: W.W. Norton, 2002, p. 275.

43. Quoted in "66 Questions and Answers About the Holocaust," www.nizkor.org/features/qar/qar00.html.

44. Wannsee Protocol, January 20, 1942, Avalon Project at Yale Law School, www.yale.edu/lawweb/avalon/imt/wannsee.html.

45. Quoted in Wistrich, *Hitler and the Holocaust*, p. 173.

46. "The Franke-Gricksch Report," Jewish Virtual Library, www.jewishvirtuallibrary.org/jsource/Holocaust/frankerep.html.

47. Quoted in "The Trial of German Major War Criminals," www.nizkor.org/hweb/imt/tgmwc/tgmwc-11/tgmwc-11-108-01.shtml.

48. Quoted in Berenbaum, *The World Must Know*, p. 139.

49. Quoted in Shirer, *The Rise and Fall of the Third Reich*, p. 969.

50. Berenbaum, *The World Must Know*, p. 95.

51. Quoted in "The Testimony of SS General Otto Ohlendorf, Einsatzgruppe D, International Military Tribunal," January 3, 1946. www.law.umkc.edu/faculty/projects/ftrials/nuremberg/Ohlentestimony.html.

52. Quoted in Benz, *The Holocaust*, p. 81.

53. Quoted in Dwork and van Pelt, *Holocaust*, p. 277.

Chapter 5:
Life and Death in Concentration Camps

54. Quoted in Lewin, *Witnesses to the Holocaust*, p. 11.

55. Quoted in "Bergen-Belsen," www.auschwitz.dk/BergenBelsen.htm.

56. Elie Wiesel, *Night*. New York: Hill & Wang, 1982, p. 34.

57. Michel Depierre, "Nordhausen Survivor," 1999. www.holocaustforgotten.com/nordhausen.htm.

58. Quoted in Gilbert, *The Holocaust*, p. 461.

59. Quoted in Claude Lanzmann, *Shoah, an Oral History of the Holocaust: The Complete Text of the Film*. New York: Pantheon, 1985, p. 165.

60. Quoted in "The True Story of Number 1067 Zygfryd Baginski—Polish Catholic Holocaust Survivor," www.holocaustforgotten.com/baginski.htm.

61. Wiesel, *Night*, p. 50.

62. Judy (Weiszenberg) Cohen, "Personal Reflections—in Camps," 2002. www3.sympatico.ca/mighty1/personal/judy.htm.

63. Quoted in Friedrich, *The Kingdom of Auschwitz*, p. 25.

64. Quoted in Gilbert, *The Holocaust*, p. 687.

65. Quoted in Lewin, *Witnesses to the Holocaust*, p. 61.

66. Quoted in Grace de Rond, "Memories to Forget," www.holocaustforgotten.com/HolocaustArtist.htm.

67. Quoted in "Kolbe, Saint of Auschwitz." www.auschwitz.dk/Kolbe.htm.

Chapter 6: Fighting Back: Rescuing Victims and Resisting Nazis

68. Quoted in Friedrich, *The Kingdom of Auschwitz*, p. 28.

69. Quoted in Joshua M. Greene and Shiva Kumar, eds., *Witness: Voices from the Holocaust*. New York: Simon & Schuster, 2000, p. 189.

70. Quoted in Gilbert, *The Holocaust*, p. 64.

71. Quoted in Berenbaum, *The World Must Know*, p. 57.

72. "Jeannine Burk," Louisiana Holocaust Survivors, www.tulane.edu/~so-inst/jeannine.html.

73. Quoted in "Remember the Village," www.auschwitz.dk/Trocme.htm.

74. Quoted in "Oskar Schindler," Jewish Virtual Library, www.jewishvirtuallibrary.org/jsource/biography/schindler.html.

75. Quoted in Soumerai and Schulz, *Daily Life During the Holocaust*, p. 204.

76. Quoted in Gilbert, *The Holocaust*, p. 484.

77. Quoted in "Resistance in the Vilna Ghetto," www.ushmm.org/research/center/resistance/awards/vilna.html.

78. "The Last Letter from Mordecai Anielewicz," April 23, 1943. Jewish Virtual Library, www.jewishvirtuallibrary.org/jsource/Holocaust/Anielewiczlet.html.

79. Quoted in Soumerai and Schulz, *Daily Life During the Holocaust*, p. 231.

80. Quoted in Gilbert, *The Holocaust*, p. 745.

81. Quoted in Lewin, *Witnesses to the Holocaust*, p. 134.

82. Quoted in Lewin, *Witnesses to the Holocaust*, p. 136.

83. Quoted in Greene and Kumar, *Witness*, p. 86.

84. Quoted in Michael T. Kaufman, "Jan Karski 1914–2000: Polish Officer and Diplomat Who Brought the Holocaust to Light," *New York Times*, July 14, 2000. www.holocaustforgotten.com/karski.html.

Chapter 7: Holocaust Survivors Make New Lives

85. Wiesel, *Night*, p. 109.

86. Quoted in Berenbaum, *The World Must Know*, p. 183.

87. Quoted in Nancy Caldwell Sorel, *The Women Who Wrote the War*. New York: Arcade, 1999, p. 349.

88. Quoted in *New York Newsday*, "Black Liberators of the Holocaust," October 22, 1992. www.members.aol.com/dignews/newsday.htm.

89. Quoted in "The Seventy-First Came to

Gunskirchen Lager," May 1945. www.re member.org/mooney/text_only.html.

90. Quoted in *New York Newsday*, "Black Liberators of the Holocaust."

91. Cohen, "Personal Reflections."

92. Quoted in Gilbert, *The Holocaust*, p. 800.

93. Quoted in Greene and Kumar, *Witness*, p. 212.

94. Cohen, "Personal Reflections."

95. Quoted in Gilbert, *The Holocaust*, p. 812.

96. Quoted in Elinor J. Brecher, *Schindler's Legacy: True Stories of the List Survivors*. New York: Penguin, 1994, p. 352.

97. Quoted in Abram L. Sachar, *The Redemption of the Unwanted: From the Liberation of the Death Camps to the Founding of Israel*. New York: St. Martin's, 1983, p. 162.

98. Quoted in Berenbaum, *The World Must Know*, p. 215.

99. Quoted in Jon Marmor, "Against All Odds," *Columns*, September 1999. www.washington.edu/alumni/columns/sept99/lantos3.html.

100. Quoted in Berenbaum, *The World Must Know*, p. 212.

101. Leah Hammerstein Silverstein, "Personal Histories Ghettos," www.ushmm.org/museum/exhibit/online/phistories/phi_ghettos_warsaw_uu.htm.

102. Quoted in Lewin, *Witnesses to the Holocaust*, p. 78.

103. "Jeannine Burk."

104. Anna W., "Excerpts from Testimonies," 2001. www.library.yale.edu/testimonies/excerpts/annaw.html.

Chapter 8:
Bringing Nazi War Criminals to Justice

105. Quoted in Doug Linder, "The Nuremberg Trials," 2000. www.law.umkc.edu/faculty/projects/ftrials/nuremberg/nurembergACCOUNT.html.

106. Quoted in Joseph E. Persico, *Nuremberg: Infamy on Trial*. New York: Viking, 1994, p. 137.

107. Quoted in Persico, *Nuremberg*, p. 137.

108. Quoted in "Testimony of Marie Claude Vaillant-Couturier," January 28, 1946. www.law.umkc.edu/faculty/projects/ftrials/nuremberg/vaillanttest.html.

109. Quoted in Linder, "The Nuremberg Trials."

110. Quoted in Avalon Project at Yale Law School, "The Nuremberg War Crimes Trials," www.yale.edu/lawweb/avalon/imt/imt.html.

111. Quoted in "The Doctor Trials: Transcript Excerpts," www.law.umkc.edu/faculty/projects/ftrials/nuremberg/NurembergDoctorTranscript.html.

112. Quoted in "The Testimony of SS General Otto Ohlendorf."

113. Simon Wiesenthal, *Justice Not Vengeance*. New York: Grove Weidenfeld, 1989, p. 50.

114. Quoted in PBS, "In His Own Words," www.pbs.org/eichmann/ownwords.htm.

115. Quoted in PBS, "In His Own Words."

116. Quoted in Berenbaum, *The World Must Know*, p. 201.

117. Quoted in John Nolan, "Court Agrees Man Was Nazi Guard," *Milwaukee Journal-Sentinel*, May 1, 2004, p. 3A.

118. Quoted in Persico, *Nuremberg*, p. 323.

Epilogue: Remembering the Holocaust

119. Shirer, *The Rise and Fall of the Third Reich*, p. 5.

120. John Paul II, "The Pope's Speech at the Yad Vashem Holocaust Memorial," March 24, 2000. www.natcath.com/NCR_Online/documents/YadVashem.htm.

121. Quoted in Ferdinando Camon, "Interview with Primo Levi," 1989. www.bryn-mawr.edu/Acads/Langs/italian/holoc/Camon_int_Levi.htm.

122. Quoted in Bart Barnes, "Artist John Komski Dies; Survived 5 Death Camps," *Washington Post*, July 23, 2002, p. A1.

123. "Dora Niederman," Louisiana Holocaust Survivors, www.tulane.edu/~so-inst/dora.html.

124. "Dora Niederman."

125. Wiesenthal, *Justice Not Vengeance*, p. 358.

126. Quoted in Friedrich, *The Kingdom of Auschwitz*, p. 102.

For Further Reading

Michael Berenbaum, *The World Must Know: The History of the Holocaust as Told in the United States Holocaust Memorial Museum.* Boston: Little, Brown, 1993. An excellent overview of all aspects of the Holocaust.

Anne Frank, *The Diary of a Young Girl: The Definitive Edition.* New York: Doubleday, 1991. The poignant words of a young Jewish girl hiding from the Nazis.

Otto Friedrich, *The Kingdom of Auschwitz.* New York: HarperCollins, 1994. A detailed, chilling account of daily life by inmates in the most notorious concentration camp.

Martin Gilbert, *Never Again: A History of the Holocaust.* New York: Universe, 2002. Filled with memorable photos, this book by one of the most acclaimed Holocaust historians explains the event in easy-to-understand mini-chapters on specific topics.

Claude Lanzmann, *Shoah, an Oral History of the Holocaust: The Complete Text of the Film.* New York: Pantheon, 1985. Text of the movie that featured interviews with Holocaust survivors.

Louis L. Snyder, *Encyclopedia of the Third Reich.* New York: McGraw-Hill, 1976. An easy guide to information about various aspects of Nazi Germany and the Holocaust.

Eve Nussbaum Soumerai and Carol D. Schulz, *Daily Life During the Holocaust.* Westport, CT: Greenwood, 1998. An interesting portrait of what happened to Holocaust victims based on their own accounts of daily life.

Elie Wiesel, *Night.* New York: Hill & Wang, 1982. A moving memoir written by a survivor.

Works Consulted

Books

Eugene Aroneanu, *Inside Concentration Camps: Eyewitness Accounts of Life in Hitler's Death Camps.* Westport, CT: Praeger, 1996. Oral histories of Holocaust survivors.

Wolfgang Benz, *The Holocaust: A German Historian Examines the Genocide.* New York: Columbia University Press, 1999. A scholarly look at the people and events that shaped the Holocaust.

Elinor J. Brecher, *Schindler's Legacy: True Stories of the List Survivors.* New York: Penguin, 1994. Interviews with individuals who were saved by Oskar Schindler.

Christopher R. Browning, with Jurgen Matthaus, *The Origins of the Final Solution: The Evolution of Nazi Jewish Policy, September 1939–March 1942.* Lincoln: University of Nebraska Press, 2004. An examination of the underlying factors that led to the Holocaust.

Alan Bullock, *Hitler: A Study in Tyranny.* New York: Smithmark, 1995. A well-documented biography of Adolf Hitler.

Michael Burleigh, *The Third Reich: A New History.* New York: Hill & Wang, 2000. Examines how Hitler came to power and created the Nazi regime that directed the Holocaust.

Lucy S. Dawidowicz, *The War Against the Jews 1933–1945.* New York: Holt, Rinehart, and Winston, 1975. The author, a relative of Holocaust victims, traces the policies that denied Jews their freedom and cost them their lives.

Deborah Dwork and Robert Jan van Pelt, *Holocaust: A History.* New York: W.W. Norton, 2002. A solid history of the Holocaust.

Martin Gilbert, *The Holocaust: A History of the Jews of Europe During the Second World War.* New York: Henry Holt, 1985. One of the most comprehensive books about the Holocaust.

Gunter Grau, *Hidden Holocaust? Gay and Lesbian Persecution in Germany 1933–45.* New York: Villiers House, 1995. This translation of a book written in German includes documents and first-person accounts of homosexual persecution during the Holocaust.

Joshua M. Greene and Shiva Kumar, eds., *Witness: Voices from the Holocaust.* New York: Simon & Schuster, 2000. This book is based on interviews from the Fortunoff Video Archive for Holocaust Testimonies at Yale University.

Michael Grynberg, ed., *Words to Outlive Us: Eyewitness Accounts from the Warsaw Ghetto.* New York: Henry Holt, 2002. Dramatic accounts of ghetto life by survivors.

Heinz Heger, *The Men with the Pink Triangles*. Los Angeles: Alyson, 1980. The author writes about being imprisoned in a concentration camp because he was a homosexual.

Adolf Hitler, *Mein Kampf*. Boston: Houghton Mifflin, 1971. Hitler's ideas in his own words.

Rhoda G. Lewin, ed., *Witnesses to the Holocaust: An Oral History*. Boston: Twayne, 1990. First-person accounts by Holocaust survivors.

Horst von Maltitz, *The Evolution of Hitler's Germany: The Ideology, the Personality, the Moment*. New York: McGraw-Hill, 1973. A scholarly examination of the philosophy underlying the Nazi regime and the Holocaust.

Joseph E. Persico, *Nuremberg: Infamy on Trial*. New York: Viking, 1994. A vivid account of the first major war crimes trial.

Abram L. Sachar, *The Redemption of the Unwanted: From the Liberation of the Death Camps to the Founding of Israel*. New York: St. Martin's, 1983. Explores what happened to Holocaust survivors at the end of World War II.

Andre Sellier, *A History of the Dora Camp*. Chicago: Ivan R. Dee, 1998. The author explains what life was like in the Dora concentration camp.

William L. Shirer, *The Rise and Fall of the Third Reich: A History of Nazi Germany*. New York: Simon & Schuster, 1960. One of the finest histories of Nazi Germany by an author who saw Hitler's rise firsthand as a reporter before World War II began.

Nancy Caldwell Sorel, *The Women Who Wrote the War*. New York: Arcade, 1999. Examines the experiences of women reporters during World War II.

Albert Speer, *Infiltration*. New York: Macmillan, 1981. A top Nazi official who served twenty years in prison, Speer explains how the *Schutzstaffel* tried to take control of the German economy.

Michael E. Stevens, ed., *Voices of the Wisconsin Past: Remembering the Holocaust*. Madison: State Historical Society of Wisconsin, 1997. Survivors who immigrated to Wisconsin tell their stories.

Simon Wiesenthal, *Justice Not Vengeance*. New York: Grove Weidenfeld, 1989. The author explains how he has tracked down Nazis since he was released from a concentration camp.

Robert S. Wistrich, *Hitler and the Holocaust*. New York: Modern Library, 2001. An interesting look at how Hitler influenced the Holocaust.

Periodicals

Bart Barnes, "Artist John Komski Dies; Survived 5 Death Camps," *Washington Post*, July 23, 2002.

Stefan Kanfer and Hugh Sidey, "The Sound Was Like a Tide Pushing Everything Before It, Remembers Richard Helms," *Time*, August 28, 1989.

John Nolan, "Court Agrees Man Was Nazi Guard," *Milwaukee Journal-Sentinel*, May 1, 2004.

Internet Sources

"Anne Levy," Louisiana Holocaust Survivors, www.tulane.edu/~so-inst/levy.html.

"Auschwitz," A Teacher's guide to the Holocaust, 2001. http://fcit.coedu.usf.edu/holocaust/resource/document/Doc Ausch.htm.

Ben S. Austin, "Homosexuals and the Holocaust." www.us-israel.org/jsource/ Holocaust/ homo.html.

Avalon Project at Yale Law School, "The Nuremberg War Crimes Trials." www.yale.edu/lawweb/avalon/imt/imt.html.

Solon Beinfeld, "The Cultural Life of the Vilna Ghetto," Simon Wiesenthal Center, 1997. http://motlc.wiesenthal.org/resources/books/annual1/chap01.html.

"Bergen-Belsen," www.auschwitz.dk/Bergen Belsen.htm.

Ferdinando Camon, "Interview with Primo Levi," 1989. www.brynmawr.edu/Acads/Langs/italian/holoc/Camon_int_Levi.htm.

Judy (Weiszenberg) Cohen, "Personal Reflections—in Camps," 2002. www3.sympatico.ca/mighty1/personal/judy.htm.

Michel Depierre, "Nordhausen Survivor," 1999. www.holocaustforgotten.com/nordhausen.htm.

Grace de Rond, "Memories to Forget," www.holocaustforgotten.com/HolocaustArtist.htm.

"The Doctor Trials: Transcript Excerpts," www.law.umkc.edu/faculty/projects/ftrials/nuremberg/NurembergDoctorTranscript.html.

"Dora Niederman," Louisiana Holocaust Survivors, www.tulane.edu/~so-inst/dora.html.

Adolf Eichmann, "The Nizkor Project," www.nizkor.org/hweb/people/e/eichmann-adolf/eichmann-004.html.

"The Franke-Gricksch Report," Jewish Virtual Library, www.jewishvirtuallibrary.org/jsource/Holocaust/frankerep.html.

"Henry Galler," Louisiana Holocaust Survivors, www.tulane.edu/~so-inst/henry.html.

Harry J. Herder Jr. "Liberation of Buchenwald," www.remember.org/witness/herder.html.

History Place, "Holocaust Timeline," 1997. www.historyplace.com/worldwar2/holocaust/timeline.html.

"Jeannine Burk," Louisiana Holocaust Survivors, www.tulane.edu/~so-inst/jeannine. html.

John Paul II, "The Pope's Speech at the Yad Vashem Holocaust Memorial," March 24, 2000. www.natcatch.com/NCR_Online/documents/YadVashem.htm.

Michael T. Kaufman, "Jan Karski 1914–2000: Polish Officer and Diplomat Who Brought the Holocaust to Light," *New York Times*, July 14, 2000. www.holocaustforgotten.com/karski.html.

"Kolbe, Saint of Auschwitz," www.auschwitz.dk/Kolbe.htm.

Jan Larsson, "Raoul Wallenberg," 1995. www.raoul-wallenberg.org.ar/english/wallening.htm.

"The Last Letter from Mordecai Anielewicz," April 23, 1943. Jewish Virtual Library, www.jewishvirtuallibrary.org/jsource/Holocaust/Anielewicz.html.

Doug Linder, "The Nuremberg Trials," 2000. www.law.umkc.edu/faculty/projects/ftrials/nuremberg/nurembergACCOUNT.html.

Jon Marmor, "Against All Odds," *Columns*, September 1999. www.washington.edu/alumni/columns/sept99/lantos3.html.

"Nazi Extermination of People with Mental Disabilities," Jewish Virtual Library, www.us-israel.org/jsource/Holocaust/mental_disabilities.html.

New York Newsday, "Black Liberators of the Holocaust," October 22, 1992. www.members.aol.com/dignews.newsday.htm.

"Oskar Schindler," Jewish Virtual Library, www.jewishvirtuallibrary.org/jsource/biography/schindler.html.

PBS, "In His Own Words," www.pbs.org/eichmann/ownwords.htm.

Dina Pronicheva, "A Survivor's Eyewitness Account," www.historyplace.com/worldwar2./holocaust/h-b-yar.htm.

"Remember the Village," www.auschwitz.dk/Trocme.htm.

"Resistance in the Vilna Ghetto," www.ushmm.org/research/center/resistance/awards/vilna.html.

Emanuel Ringelblum, "Life in the Warsaw Ghetto," A Teacher's Guide to the Holocaust, 2001. http://fcit.coedu.usf.edu/holocaust/resource/document/DocRing1.htm.

"The Seventy-First Came to Gunskirchen Lager," May 1945. www.remember.org/mooney/text_only.html.

William L. Shulman, "Anatomy of a Ghetto," Holocaust Resource Center and Archives, www.qcc.cuny.edu/HRCA/news/anatomy_of_ghetto_pl. htm.

"Sigmund Boraks," Louisiana Holocaust Survivors, www.tulane.edu/~so-inst/sigmund.html.

Leah Hammerstein Silverstein, "Personal Histories Ghettos," www.ushmm.org/museum/exhibit/online/phistories/phi_ ghettos_warsaw_uu.htm.

"66 Questions and Answers About the Holocaust." www.nizkor.org/features/qar/qar00.html.

"Testimony of Marie Claude Vaillant-Couturier," January 28, 1946. www.law.umkc.edu/faculty/projects/ftrials/nuremberg/vaillanttest.html.

"The Testimony of SS General Otto Ohlendorf, Einsatzgruppe D, International Military Tribunal," January 3, 1946. www.law.umkc.edu/faculty/projects/ftrials/nuremberg/Ohlen-testimony.html.

"Treblinka Deathcamp," www.auschwitz.dk/Treblinka.htm.

"The Trial of German Major War Criminals," www.nizkor.org/hweb/imt/tgmwc/tgmwc-11/tgmwc-11-108-01. shtml.

"The True Story of Number 1067 Zygfryd Baginski—Polish Catholic Holocaust Survivor," www.holocaustforgotten.com/baginski.htm.

Fernand Van Horen, "How a Drawing Saved My Life," www.jewishgen.org/ForgottenCamps/Witnesses/HornEng.html.

Anna W., "Excerpts from Testimonies," 2001. www.library.yale.edu/testimonies/excerpts/annaw.html.

Wannsee Protocol, January 20, 1942, Avalon Project at Yale Law School, www. yale.edu/lawweb/avalon/imt/wannsee.htm.

Web Sites

Jewish Virtual Library (www.jewishvirtuallibrary.org/jsource/holo.html). This Web site created by the American-Israeli Cooperative Enterprise is an excellent source.

Simon Wiesenthal Center (www.wiesenthal.com). Contains an extensive collection of material on the Holocaust as well as the hunt for Nazi war criminals.

A Teacher's Guide to the Holocaust (http://fcit.coedu.usf.edu/holocaust/default.htm). This site by the Florida Center for Instructional Technology has a wide range of good information on the Holocaust.

United States Holocaust Memorial Museum (www.ushmm.org). A Web site by the museum in Washington, D.C.

Index

Picture Credits

About the Author

Michael V. Uschan has written more than forty books, including *The Korean War*, for which he won the 2002 Council of Wisconsin Writers Juvenile Nonfiction Award. Uschan began his career as a writer and editor with United Press International, a wire service that provides stories to newspapers, radio, and television. Journalism is sometimes called "history in a hurry." Uschan considers writing history books a natural extension of the skills he developed during his many years as a journalist. He and his wife, Barbara, reside in the Milwaukee suburb of Franklin, Wisconsin.